C.S. PEIRCE
Categories to Constantinople

LOUVAIN PHILOSOPHICAL STUDIES 13

C.S. PEIRCE
CATEGORIES TO CONSTANTINOPLE

PROCEEDINGS
OF THE INTERNATIONAL SYMPOSIUM ON PEIRCE
LEUVEN 1997

EDITED BY JAAP VAN BRAKEL AND MICHAEL VAN HEERDEN

Leuven University Press

Uitgegeven met steun van de Universitaire Stichting van België en het Francqui Fonds.

©1998 Leuven University Press / Presses Universitaires de Louvain / Universitaire Pers Leuven
Blijde-Inkomststraat 5, B-3000 Leuven (Belgium)

ISBN 90 6186 939 0
D/1998/1869/77

CONTENTS

ABBREVIATIONS

The following commonly accepted abbreviations are used throughout this volume for citations from the various editions of Peirce's works.

CP   *Collected Papers of Charles Sanders Peirce*, edited by C. Hartshorne and P. Weiss (volumes 1-6), and A. Burks (volumes 7-8) (Cambridge, MA: Harvard University Press, 1931-1958), followed by volume and paragraph number and, when appropriate, year in which the passage was written.

HP   *Historical Perspectives on Peirce's Logic of Science: A History of Science*, edited by Carolyn Eisele, 2 volumes (Berlin: Mouton-De Gruyter, 1985), followed by volume and page number.

MS   Peirce manuscripts in Houghton Library at Harvard University, followed by a number identified in Richard R. Robin, *Annotated Catalogue of the Papers of Charles S. Peirce* (Amherst, MA: University of Massachusetts Press, 1967), and, when given, a year and page number in which passage was written.

N   *Charles Sanders Peirce: Contributions to The Nation*, edited by Kenneth Laine Ketner and James Edward Cook, 4 volumes (Lubbock, TX: Texas Tech University Press, 1975-1987), followed by volume and page number.

NEM   *The New Elements of Mathematics by Charles S. Peirce*, edited by Carolyn Eisele, 4 volumes in 5 books (The Hague: Mouton, 1976), followed by volume and page number.

PW   *Semiotic and Significs: The Correspondence between Charles S. Peirce and Victoria Lady Welby*, edited by Charles S. Hardwick (Bloomington, IN: Indiana University Press, 1977), followed by page number.

SW   *Charles S. Peirce: Selected Writings (Values in a Universe of Chance)*, edited by P. Wiener (New York: Dover Publications, 1958), followed by page number.

W   *Writings of Charles S. Peirce: A Chronological Edition*, edited by Max H. Fisch *et al.* (Bloomington, IN: Indiana University Press, 1982-1993), followed by volume and page number.

ABOUT THE AUTHORS

Guy Debrock is professor of philosophy at the Faculty of Science in the Catholic University of Nijmegen (The Netherlands). His chief area of research is the philosophy of Peirce and the theory of information.

Jaap van Brakel studied chemical engineering and philosophy. He has taught at universities in The Netherlands and Canada and is currently professor at the Higher Institute of Philosophy of the Catholic University of Leuven in Belgium.

Luciana Floridi studied philosophy in Rome and England. Presently he is Research Fellow in philosophy at Wolfson College, Oxford and lecturer in philosophy at Jesus College and St Anne's College, University of Oxford.

Michael van Heerden studied social science, philosophy and theology in South Africa. Presently he is a doctoral student at the Catholic University of Leuven, doing research on the notion of instinct in Peirce.

Ralf Müller is assistant professor in philosophy at Fordham University in New York, United States of America. He studied philosophy, history, German and mathematics in Germany and has been a visiting scholar in England.

Menno Hulswit studied biology and philosophy. He is assistant professor in philosophy at the Catholic University of Nijmegen and is presently writing a book on causation in Peirce.

Els Wouters is a doctoral student at the University of Antwerp in Belgium. She is doing research on the inferences in the detective story. Recently, she has obtained the mandate of Research Assistant of the Fund of Scientific Research - Flanders.

Gérard Deledalle studied philosophy at the Sorbonne in Paris, France. He was Research Fellow at Columbia University, New York and attaché at the Centre National de la Recherche Scientifique in Paris. He was head of the philosophy departments of the universities of Tunis, Perpignon and Libreville. Presently he is vice-president of the International Association for Semiotic Studies and member of the Advisory Board of the Peirce Edition Project, Indiana University.

INTRODUCTION

It had been the life-long ambition of Charles Sanders Santiago Peirce (1839-1914) to produce a systematic testimony of his overall philosophical program. A dream which became all the more urgent for him as the years of his life closed in on him and he found himself more and more isolated from the academic community of the late 19th and early 20th century. Much of his philosophical writings were, however, never published in his own time, nor read by the public at large. While being the acknowledged father of American Pragmatism, he is also sometimes rather enigmatically called the 'philosopher's philosopher' or the 'neglected argument'. The reasons given for this neglect of Peirce (both during his lifetime and after) range from allusions to his eccentric ways, to suggestions of academic 'foul play' on the part of his contemporaries and those who might have disseminated his ideas after his life.

His contributions to contemporary philosophy, nonetheless, can be felt in almost every field of inquiry. His contributions to logical theory are numerous and profound. Working on the logic of relations, he built on the ideas of De Morgan and influenced Schröder, and through him, Peano, Russell and Lowenheim, to mention just a few. Some of his other logical contributions include his quantification theory, propositional logic and work on Boolean algebra. However, it is not only in the field of logic that his presence endures. In the field of experimental psychology, it appears as if Peirce was the first American to grasp the importance of the work of Wundt and Fechner. Through her contacts with Peirce, Christine Ladd-Franklin (America's first female psychologist) was to have an enduring interest in logical and visual processing. Peirce's philosophic architectonic includes as well much original work in the philosophy of science. His discussions on abduction, for example, were very influential on the thought of Eco; and the notion of the 'would-be' and the dispositional interpretation of probability had a prodigious outcome in the thought of Popper and others. We find in Peirce's philosophy of mind, evolution, and epistemology many contemporary parallels. Two are particularly worth mentioning. First, his discussions on the dynamics of doubt and belief and his ideas on the community of inquirers were influential on the thought of Mead and Habermas. Second, far-reaching has been Peirce's notion of the end of inquiry as the pragmatic theory of truth. Many contemporary thinkers have acknowledged their indebtedness to Peirce, people such as Mc Mullin,

Putnam and Quine. For many others, the influence has doubtlessly been more indirect and subtle.

While there had been some pioneers in pragmatic thought outside America during Peirce's own lifetime, as is evidenced from his letters to Calderoni and the other Italian pragmatists, when the publication of the *Collected Papers* began in 1931, an international interest in Peirce gradually blossomed. However, even today there remain some areas of neglect. This neglect is evidenced particularly in what has been referred to as Peirce's 'white elephant', or his metaphysical and cosmological thought. Even a cursory reading of Peirce will show that he was convinced of two things: first, that every scientific or philosophical system is necessarily undergirded by a metaphysical system, albeit scorned or ignored; second, that his own metaphysical thought was central to his philosophy and a vital tool in releasing its elixir. Still, even had he not made these points clear, the question should be raised whether one can, without examining these two areas, give a comprehensive portrayal of the thought of this multi-faceted thinker.

Perhaps part of the present neglect has wider implications and is indicative of the debate within what could be called the 'history of philosophy versus the systematic philosophy' dispute. Mc Intyre, for example, presents this tangle in terms of a dilemma: there are always elements of any philosophy of the past which oppose transportation and these tend to become ignored; whereas, if we do read texts carefully and respect the idiosyncratic and unique elements, what emerges is an interesting 'museum piece', with little relevance to life today. A more moderate exposition of the problem would admit that there *should* always be divergences in the two approaches, so as both to preserve the original unity of ideas (history of philosophy), while also highlighting the subjective reconstructions and contributions of the present (systematic philosophy). However, even if we were more extreme and said that the two approaches were incommensurable, this position *should* imply some type of objective understanding of the two paradigms involved. While we undoubtedly always approach another philosophy from our own unique paradigm, the 'fusion of horizons' (as Gadamer would call it) can only be intensified and broadened if we ensure a measure of objectivity by evaluating the other horizon within the unity of its own concerns and the context of its time.

A SYMPOSIUM ON PEIRCE

It was the express aim of the International Symposium on Peirce, organized by the Higher Institute of Philosophy (Catholic University of Leuven), to examine Peirce's thought in terms of both its historical integrity and in the application of his thought to current problems. The speakers who were invited were asked to keep both approaches in mind when choosing their topics and the nature of their presentations. What emerged was an interesting spectrum of talks. While all of them have made contemporary applications of Peirce's thought, there is also an underlying respect for what has been called the 'ecstatic naturalism' of Peirce (his metaphysical and cosmological insights) as well as the historical context in which it emerged. The symposium was held between the 23rd and 25th of May, 1997, and the talks were presented in no particular order of preference. When the suggestion was made, however, that these should be presented in a volume, the latter question came to the fore together with that of an appropriate title. It was then decided that the two most general talks should mark the inauguration and completion of the presentation. The first paper, thus, presents various insights into, and the development of, the Peircean categories; while the last paper reflects on these categories in their application to Peirce's understanding of God and the development of the christian doctrine of the Trinity. Since the latter makes special reference to the different councils of the early church, particularly that of Constantinople, the title of the volume naturally presented itself. Having settled the question of a title and broad outline for the order of the contributions, it was then decided to place them in order of their application, from the most general to the most specific. Hence, the present sequence.

OVERVIEW OF PAPERS

The first paper, then, is entitled: 'Peirce's Category of Secondness and Information', the last part of the title being "the nearly hidden agenda". Beginning with a reference to two examples taken from quantum mechanics and neurobiology, Debrock shows how the basic categories of our western discourse have become the "proverbial old bags into which it is very unwise to pour new wine"; what is called for is a *new list of categories*, which is precisely what Peirce attempted to do when drafting his list of the three categories of Firstness, Secondness and Thirdness.

While Peirce's list began as an extension of his logic, the paper shows clearly that the function of the categories and their application opened up in the thought of Peirce to eventually including "any and all appearance". This is illustrated in three ways. First, there is a chronological comparison of the way in which Peirce conceived their function, which broadens finally into an ontological conception. Second, there is a thorough analysis of the various contexts in which the categories were used and developed by Peirce (pragmatic, logic of relations, psychological, evolution, phenomenology, metaphysics) and some of the historical influences that spurred their growth. Finally, there is also a chronological table that shows the development of Peirce's nomenclature of the categories. This table shows that it was Peirce's category of Secondness that underwent the most radical revision over the years. While no-one would dispute the centrality of Thirdness in giving 'definiteness' to every appearance, "such definiteness can only *be* in respect to the element of Secondness". Debrock is, thus, brought to the conclusion that at the heart of Peirce's doctrine of the categories, is the category of Secondness. When describing the categories in a 'nutshell', Debrock makes the intriguing assertion of a *Peircean Ontological Principle* (which has remarkable echoes in Whitehead): "If there is no Secondness, there is nothing at all ... [but] all three categories are always necessary elements of appearance".

Having established an exposé of the categories, the relevance of them to the concept of information is now briefly explored. If in-*form*-ation is taken in its widest meaning as "an activity whereby form arises", then it is really an informative *event*. Further, each event has three poles: *how* it occurred, *that* it occurred, *what difference* its occurrence makes. Since these three poles correspond exactly to Peirce's categories of Firstness, Secondness and Thirdness, "information is the one concept that perfectly fits the specifications of Peirce's categories". If our old bags are showing wear and tear, then perhaps it is time to take Peirce seriously and provide a *new list of categories* based in the insights of Peirce, but translated into the *new* language of information.

'Peirce's Natural Kinds', is the title of the second paper of this volume. Beginning with a summary of the lack of consensus (and general confusion) within the philosophy of science today as to what should be described as a *natural kind*, van Brakel is able to show that depictions vary from genetic types, to all classes within the gambit of cultural life. Clearly, the lack of consensus is traceable to differing *definitions* of the concept, as well as to the *interpretation* of the "meaning of terms" within definitions. Peirce's *real kinds* and *natural classes* are his entré into the contemporary debate. Van Brakel in his paper addresses two questions to the insights of Peirce: "first, what kinds, if any, are excluded from" the definitions of Peirce; and second, whether Peirce's definitions of real kinds and natural classes lead down "the primrose path of eliminativism".

Apropos of the first question, van Brakel shows that Peirce's answers are not always consistent; and, while the idea of the 'ultimate conception' is central to them, even that is open to either a pluralistic or eliminativistic interpretation. If we appeal to a 'general shared intuition', for example, in what will finally prevail as a natural kind (as Peirce clearly did), then the problem lies in placing the boundaries to *general* and *shared*. With reference to different *cultural* kinds, van Brakel is able to lever open the 'imperialism' of those who might put the boundaries for shared and general at some reductionist or scientific interest (eliminativism), to the exclusion of other legitimate human concerns.

This then brings the discussion to the second question. Peirce's conceptions of real kinds and natural classes might well lead down the path of eliminativism, if there were not an equally valid pluralistic interpretation of them in which the "distinction between natural and non-natural classes disappears". This conclusion can be reached in four ways. First, because Peirce describes the ultimate conception of a natural kind in terms of the "power of working out results in this world" (CP 1.220), which would apply to most classes across the board. Second, Peirce's notions of *common sense* and *fallibilism*, imply that every department of inquiry: from metaphysics, to science, to everyday experience, has a stake in determining what is *natural*. Third, as Peirce emphasizes the *instinctive* base of all progress in scientific inquiry, science cannot claim any *rational* superiority to other conceptions which are equally well-founded. Lastly, Peirce's subordination of scientific inquiry to ethics and esthetics means that the former is rooted inextricably within an open "social principle" (CP 2. 654).

In the finale to this discussion, van Brakel recommends that perhaps the Peircean conceptual scheme suggests, rather than the cul de sac of eliminativism, the "hope" for a continuing pluralism in which open exchange and tolerance will be the greatest incentives for human advancement.

Since *fallibilism* was a consideration for showing that all classes must have a hearing in the contemporary debate on what is natural, perhaps we could ask what are its *limits*. The third paper of this volume sets out to do that in a provocative title adapted from Oscar Wilde: 'The Importance of Being Earnest: Scepticism and the Limits of Fallibilism in Peirce'. While scepticism is the type of "embarrassing company any thoughtful epistemology" would rather avoid, the question is posed as to how epistemology is able to avoid "sceptical questions" in order to lift itself out of dogmatism and arm itself with "the conceptual resources necessary to avoid being led astray by nonsensical doubts". Floridi has no doubts that Peirce is an anti-sceptic, but while his fallibilism succeeds in achieving the just mentioned projects, it does this "only on account of the metaphysical price his philosophy is ready to pay".

Peirce's different depictions of scepticism through the years are explained with the help of a chronological table showing how they ranged from extreme Cartesian doubt (faked scepticism) to a more constructive, moderate assessment of scepticism - provided that it be genuinely in pursuit of the advancement of knowledge. Floridi then goes on to show how it is the second assessment of scepticism that is vital for the preservation of other areas of Peirce's thought. First, because it is indispensable in Peirce's critique of the different methods of fixing belief and in showing that the scientific method is the most authentic way of "being earnest in the pursuit of knowledge". Second, while rejecting that perfect knowledge is attainable, Peirce nonetheless held to an asymptotic approach to it, which is facilitated by investigation and the *critical* exchange among the "community of investigators".

However, the question remains whether Peirce's fallibilistic hypothesis is able to undermine *extreme* scepticism. In a depiction of the components of Peirce's fallibilism (ontological, epistemic, *consensus omnium*, anthropological and perceptual), Floridi shows how each is defective without the support of the other arguments. Peirce is, thus, caught in a type of circularity which is reminiscent of "scholastic monism": founded on a strong metaphysic that assumes the "reliable communication between being and mind", it has to reject the "static dichotomy between man and a mechanized, soul-less universe". A metaphysic which, in the end, has just to be *assumed* in order to defend its fundamental postulates. In conclusion to his portrayal of the dilemma facing Peirce, Floridi admits that this assumption in Peirce does allow his fallibilism to be a form of realism, rather than instrumentalism. Without a similar assumption, all systems of fallibilism "stand before the world as a separate, constantly revisable manifold of laws", and science can only be said to be "indeterminately linked with reality". But, says Floridi, perhaps after all the latter is the more authentic "trench" in which to *be*?

But did Peirce ever give an illustration of, or defense for, his strong form of monistic metaphysics? The answer to this question brings us to the fourth paper of the volume: 'Reason and Instinct'. As Peirce's thought matured he became more and more convinced that both the possibility of conscious experience and the ability to reason critically were based in instinct. Van Heerden begins his paper by asking whether the concept of instinct is not perhaps one of those 'old bags' spoken about in the first paper. Many contemporary writers see no utility in a reason/instinct divide as there are no infallible criteria by which to distinguish the two. Peirce definitely anticipated these objections in noting that the two can never be divided, but that the most one can do is place all actions along a continuum of self-control. Van Heerden notes that, for Peirce, as the simplest instinct of the reflex arc becomes more and more specific in living forms, it gives birth to "a hierarchy of instincts and emerging levels of self-control". The first hierarchy is a simple interaction between what Peirce conceives of as the *selfish* and *social* instincts, but these in turn form the foundation of numerous other *cycles* of association (habits), which interact in patterns of inclusion, exclusion and intersection to form the scope of consciousness in each living form. For Peirce these interactions are at the basis of human consciousness which is embodied in the three elements of Primisense, Altersense and Medisense. The two fundamental types of association, as is echoed in Hume and many other philosophers of the mind, are associations of resemblance and contiguity. Making use of Peirce's metaphor of the lake (CP 7. 547), van Heerden is able to show that the different patterns of "buoyancy" which both inhibit and facilitate the rising of associational patterns to the surface (consciousness) are, first and foremost, the instincts that undergird human nature. These are governed by an overall *principle of subsidiarity*, that dictates that what should rise to the next level of self-control are only those actions and 'thoughts' which cannot be resolved or dealt with at lower levels. However, the self-control that emerges in human nature from its instincts yields a novel ability to build up new associational patterns that are not based only in experience or accidental associations, but also in Medisense: conscious, critical reasoning. This ability, in turn, is the infrastructure which undergirds our aptitude to use symbols and language. Van Heerden shows how Peirce conceived of the social instincts as being "more sympathetic to reason", because these give us the facility for "scenario-spinning" and "diagrammatic manipulation" within the imagination. The latter also allow for the "whole enterprise of mathematical and logical thought".

But what about imagination and memory? How does Peirce account for the new *creative* associations that characterize the progress of human thought? Peirce's answer would be that it is in the metaphysical nature of all habits to be states of feeling. In humans, this is shown in Primisense (conscious feeling); but, since all habits have a feeling-component, they can affect each other in new ways (imagination) and also call up other associational habits that have a resemblance to them (memory). Perhaps a puerile suggestion, but maybe not so bizarre when one considers that a central *motive* state has the observed properties of "perpetuating itself, evoking general activity, and "priming" and emitting specific reactions".

What Peirce conceived of as being diagrammatic manipulation brings us to the next paper of this volume: 'Peirce's Existential Graphs: First Inquiries Towards a Proper Interpretation'. Some facts and some stories provide the opening for Müller in his portrayal of the EG (existential graphs) of Peirce. Since one of the virtues of EG over first-order logic is their "interactive" ability, the presentation begins our "expedition" by asking us to interact directly with a demonstration of the methods of transformation and the conventions that govern these in the thought of Peirce. After this first-hand experience of the EG, the paper sets to find out exactly what the EG are. This is done through the critical discussion of three other analogous attempts to graphically portray the processes of human thought: the graphical system of Sowa; the conceptual graph workbench of the University of Adelaide; and the hyperproof project of Barwise and Etchemendy. The merits of EG over first-order logical systems that survive this criticism seem to be three: their "expressive" power, their "interactive" capacities, and their ability to be "directly manipulated" (which makes them better pedagogical tools). Müller then turns back to the statements of Peirce as to the character and purpose of the EG, and strangely enough the same epistemic advantages emerge from his definitions. What is particularly evident of EG is that they are a system of "homophoric representation, or, to put it in other words, EG mimic the dynamics of argumentation, they display 'thinking *in actu*' ".

In Peirce's thought, formal thinking (or argumentation) is always characterized as comprising of three actions: *colligation* (putting together facts), *experimentation and observation*, and *generalization* (CP 7.276). Since EG do not give the conventions for the first and last of these elements, Müller makes the observation that the "interpreter of the graphs appears to be an integral part of the total setup necessary to simulate reasoning", and this seemingly also keeps "a path open for an integration of non-necessary reasoning into the logic of EG". Müller, then, in a short diversion shows that, because of the former, EG are not to be seen as standing alone in the illustration of human reasoning in Peirce's philosophy, but as an integral part of his semeiosis and his proof of pragmaticism. Because all three are interdependent, Peirce can be seen as anticipating the contemporary dynamic trend in logic that "does not only comprise approaches to semantics that focus on action structure, but, also, theories that take a situated agent as the starting point of semantical considerations". Further, because of their agent-based dependence, Müller makes the suggestion that EG and other graphical systems cannot (independently of the human agent) model the possibility of error, which is "an indication of any logic's limits and ... the main obstacle for that branch of artificial intelligence called logic-AI".

As this is a "first inquiry" into the correct philosophical understanding of the EG of Peirce, any further research has to show that they are both integral to his system as a whole and part of his *dynamic* understanding of reasoning. Two points that have emerged with clarity throughout this paper. But, what has also emerged is that all graphs (including EG) are essentially limited: giving only "general notations by which different logics can be modelled"; but, perhaps more importantly, no "notation can make philosophical reflection superfluous".

If EG are an integral part of the philosophy of Peirce, and are part of his overall semeiotic project, it would be beneficial to examine aspects of the latter in more detail. This brings us to the sixth paper of this volume: 'Semeiotic, Causation, and Semeiotic Causation'. At the conclusion of the first paper, mention was made of the notion of information. We also saw that underpinning its meaning was the notion of an activity through which *form* arises. A question, then, naturally ensues as to the origins of any form. For Peirce, form is irreducibly a question of Thirdness, final causality, or semeiosis (the processes of sign-action). Hulswit sets himself the goal of examining two of these three elements. These make up the contents of his title and the aim of his paper is to see how they are intertwined in the thinking of Peirce. The first part of the paper examines what is generally meant by semeiosis. Beginning with a portrayal of Peirce's understanding of a *sign*, its *object* and the *interpretant*, Hulswit notes that the key to the comprehension of these is to see that the relationship between them is "irreducibly triadic". Further, since "to act as a sign is to determine an interpretant", and "every sign involves a virtually infinite series of interpretants", semeiosis is a "teleological process directed toward a complete manifestation of the object, in which the object seems to function as the final cause".

The second element of the title is causation. For Peirce, every action has three components: a final cause, an efficient cause and an element of chance. Every triadic action (or revelation of Thirdness) in Peirce is associated with *intelligence*, because intelligent action "involves the causation of one event as a *means* to another event". But this does not imply "backward causation", rather the *final* cause determines the *general purpose* and overall structure of an action. Nor does this rule out novelty, for while every act involves a component of final causality, there is also a component of chance, and both are manifested through the workings of efficient causality. As it were, final causes are forms or "general types that triadically determine causal processes", and efficient causes are the various concrete instances of those processes which exhibit both form and formlessness (originality).

After having clarified these points, Hulswit sets himself to explore how the two are related. While *signs* need not be "triadically produced" (as, for example, smoke is not produced as a *means* to any end of the fire, yet still functions as a *sign* of fire); Hulswit contends that, nonetheless, all *interpretants* are necessarily produced triadically (as the interpretation that where there is smoke, there must be a fire, can only come about when the two elements are brought together by a *third* component, the interpreter). By means of two diagrams, Hulswit is first able to show that the production of any *final* interpretant (the interpretation "toward which ... semeiosis tends") is a manifestation of final causality. Since it is causality in the context of semeiosis, Hulswit coins the term of *semeiotic causality*. However, does the production of *emotional* and *energetic* (actions that follow from any sign) interpretations also imply final causality? A musical performance and the marching of a squadron after an officer's command are provided as suitable examples of each in which to explore an answer. These are shown to confirm the suspicion that even here there is semeiotic causality at play. Chance is displayed in the fact that "every sign ... does not present a complete representation of its object" and, thus, it permits "a latitude of different" interpretations.

The paper concludes with an assessment of certain problems within the notion of semeiotic causation. The first is the question whether all actions can fit into the scheme of semeiotic causation presented in the paper. The second is even more fundamental. If all causal processes are of a semeiotic nature, then one seems justified in concluding that the latter is a more basic notion in Peirce than the former. But, then to try to explain semeiosis in terms of final causality is "putting the cart before the horse".

In the course of this paper it was noted that a sign need not necessarily be produced triadically. One example given by Hulswit is that of "a thief who unwittingly leaves behind a fingerprint". It would then be the interpretation of the detective that is triadic and links the two together. This, then, opens up another dimension that is dealt with in the seventh paper of this volume: 'Creative Abduction in the Detective Story'. The question of 'detection', or "the logical means used by fictional detectives" to come to an understanding of the initial crime (as it were, after the fact) is the context within which this paper explores Peirce's notion of *abduction*. Wouters begins this exposition by noting the similarities between the genre of detective novels and the processes of semeiotics. The detective, when confronted with the *clues* at the scene of the crime and elsewhere, is automatically caught up in a semeiotic process "that consists in attaching the right value to these signs" so that the "truth of what has happened will finally come to light". But what enables the detective to make any inferences at all from these clues? Wouters shows that this question has often been addressed by reference to Sherlock Holmes and as to whether he uses deduction (as he is so want to proclaim), induction or abduction. By showing the differing positions of authors who have separately emphasized one of these logical activities, Wouters is also able to bring into focus the nuances in the activities themselves. It was Umberto Eco who made the link between the fictional detective's activities and Peirce's notion of abduction, particularly since Peirce stresses the fact that abduction is the only logical method of reasoning in which the invention of new theories can come about. Abduction is a "mode of conjectural interpretation, which requires a certain amount of intuition or feeling", which cannot be called reasonable. This, in turn, has lead many writers to comment on the contradictory nature of abduction both in detection and scientific practice. To further explore the nature of abduction, Wouters now makes a comparison between different fictional detectives and their methods. What emerges clearly from this is: first, since they do not operate in the same way, their "inferences cannot be labelled in the same way"; and, second, even with abduction, sub-types can be discerned. Eco provides three sub-types, but Wouters goes on the show (with reference to Peirce's definitions of abduction) that Peirce's understanding of abduction "is inextricably bound up with creativity", or the creative sub-type (to use Eco's terminology). That creative abduction is the "most hazardous type" is illustrated in the context again of two detectives from fiction.

To conclude her analysis, Wouters ends on a more sober note by emphasizing that, since the illustration of abduction was done within the framework of *fiction* (which is a selective representation of real life), the detective or scientist outside of books, can at best only approximate the abductive imagination, operation and success of the fictional detective.

The final paper of this volume closes the circle of discussion by taking us back to Peirce's categories. The title itself: 'Peirce, Theologian', should be illustrative of the 'creative' nature of the application of these categories both within the writings of Peirce, as well as the article. Beginning with some interesting biographical details, Deledalle is able to sketch briefly the pertinent details of Peirce's pilgrimage of faith and how he came to accept the christian doctrine of the Trinity within his triadic structure of categories. Turning to Peirce's famous article on musement and the reality of God, Deledalle illustrates how musement corresponds to the activity of Firstness; and Firstness, in turn, if seen as "coextensive with possibility", means the *reality* of God. The subtlety of Peirce's argument can only be appreciated if one keeps in mind that he drew a sharp distinction between reality and existence. Since possibility exemplifies perfectibility, God as first is *real* perfectibility and so gives birth to *existence* (Secondness), in which God's reality can be *realized* though existence becoming *more real* (Thirdness). Musement, as the activity of Firstness, puts us into contact with the *possibility* of God (abduction), which is ratified in our reflection on *existence* (induction), and the concrete *processes* of cosmic advance (deduction). Deledalle makes the suggestion, therefore, that Peirce's neglected argument for God, is unique - as all others, from Anselm onwards, have focussed on the latter two processes of thought (induction and deduction) in founding their arguments for God, whereas Peirce focusses on the creative process of abduction in founding his.

Having established the broad outline of Peirce's doctrine of God, Deledalle then turns to illustrate it with reference to the development of the christian doctrine of the Trinity. The differences in interpretation between the east and west are illustrated as reflecting historical, political, conceptual, and linguistic idiosyncrasies. This is done with reference to the different councils that led to the refinement of the terms of the doctrine as well as its overall formulation. What is particularly interesting in this section is how Deledalle is able to show that, at core, the enduring dispute between eastern and western conceptions is primarily a question of whether one approaches the mystery of *God in Three* from the angle of God's diversity, so as to establish God's unity (eastern approach), or whether one begins by assuming God's unity and then moves to the diversity (western approach). Peirce is closer in his understanding of God to the former. Deledalle's succinct summary of Peirce's position, which closes his discussion, is worth replicating here: "the Son proceeds from the Father out of time, but precedes him in time ... The *procession* moves downward; what it gains in multiplicity, it loses in unity: the Father is first, the Son is second, the Holy Spirit is third".

PEIRCE'S CATEGORY OF SECONDNESS AND INFORMATION

GUY DEBROCK

Very wretched is the notion of [the categories] that can be conveyed in one lecture. They must grow up in the mind, under the hot sunshine of hard thought, daily, bright, well-focussed, and well-aimed thought; and you must have patience, for long time is required to ripen the fruit. They are no inventions of mine. Were they so, that would be sufficient to condemn them. Confused notions of these elements appear in the first infancy of philosophy, and they have never entirely been forgotten.

(CP 1.521 [1903d])

1. AIMS OF THIS PAPER

The nearly hidden agenda of this paper is the attempt to interpret Peirce's 'New List of Categories' in terms of a theory of information. I shall briefly allude to it at the end of this composition. The more immediate purpose of the paper is to show how Peirce's doctrine of categories developed from a purely logical concept to a concept pertaining to any and all appearance, in every sense of the word.

My paper will consist of four parts. In the first introductory part, I shall briefly try to show the relevance of my attempt. In the second and most lengthy part, I shall deal with the development of Peirce's doctrine of the categories. In a third, and much shorter part, I shall argue that, although Peirce's concern was always primarily the category of Thirdness, the heart of his doctrine is his category of Secondness. Moreover, I will attempt to show that, if Secondness of the genuine variety is interpreted in the spirit of Peirce's writings on the subject, there can be no doubt that his doctrine of categories is really primarily a doctrine regarding *events*. In the fourth and last part, I shall, again briefly, try to show in what way Peirce's doctrine of categories may be relevant to a theory of information.

2. THE RELEVANCE OF THE TOPIC

As we are approaching the end of the century, the intellectual mood of our culture is marked by a certain polarity. On the one hand, there is the philosophical mood which is increasingly skeptical or relativistic, and there is the scientific mood which is - generally speaking - upbeat, optimistic, full of confidence. There is probably something to be said for each of these two poles. But we can hardly be satisfied with a mere acknowledgment of the tension. We are also interested in resolving it. And if the tension is to be resolved, it may be good to ask for the reason of this tension.

There are circumstances in which the language in which we usually express the things we are doing, no longer fulfills its function. Thus, a language sometimes may be said to reach its end. The symptoms of such ends are most manifest when the strain is felt in the use of terms which are so basic that we could not speak to each other publicly without using them. Such concepts Aristotle called *categories* (i.e. concepts we use 'on the public place'). A really new language requires a *new list of categories*. Thus, the tension to which I referred may be a symptom that we are badly in need of a change of language, and, therefore, that we are badly in need of a new list of categories. There is every indication that the categories of our western discourse simply have become the proverbial old bags into which it is very unwise to pour new wine.

Let me mention two examples which, to my mind, are symptomatic of the wear and tear of the old bags. I should preface the first example by saying that I am not in any way a physicist and, thus, I would very much like to stand corrected if what I say makes no sense to those who are. It is well known that quantum mechanics has been hugely successful, both scientifically and technically. It has long ceased to be a purely theoretical invention of theoretical physicists; it has become the mainstay of modern chemistry and, through biochemistry, it has become the key to many innovations in the fields of medicine and pharmacy. Many people literally owe their being alive to the discovery of quantum mechanics. Yet, in spite of this great success, scientists are still at a loss when it comes to an interpretation of what may be called the 'sacred formulas' which form the core of the discipline. Every university student in chemistry has some knowledge of the Schrödinger equation, yet very few can clearly express what it means. In fact, there is only agreement about the fact that there is a great amount of disagreement regarding the interpretation of the theory. The reason for this is that, as soon as the formulas which are expressed in mathematical language are explained in terms of ordinary language, the so-called paradoxes raise their heads so profusely that one wonders at the almost arcane or near mystical associations which those explanations entail. Those explanations make use of analogies in which the main role is played by cats or particles, a fact which suggests that the things of which quantum mechanics speaks are entities in the same sense in which we speak of entities in ordinary language. In other words, we read the theory through glasses that were made for a description of a world which has little in common with a world which is inherently linked to the mathematical language in which it is expressed; a world which is as invisible to those glasses as the refraction of infra-red light is invisible to our ordinary eyes.

The second example I borrow from an article in which a description was given of some of the research on memory that is going on in neurobiology. In the article, one scientist says:

> The self is not a little person inside the brain. It is a perpetually recreated neurobiological state, so continuously and consistently reconstructed that the owner never knows it is being remade. (Geary [1997])

Such a quote is typical of an attempt at expressing in a certain language something which, by virtue of the very language spoken, cannot be said. What does it mean to say that something is the owner of the self that he is? And can not what he says of the self be said of the brain itself?

If it should prove correct that many problems of interpretation are the result of the deficiencies of our language and, if it is correct to say that a language is largely determined by its basic categories, then it would follow that the search for a new language must begin with the search for a new list of categories.

This is precisely what Peirce did when, in 1867, he published his obscure article entitled: 'On a New List of Categories', which he later would call his "one contribution to philosophy" (CP 8.213). He never intended to say that he proposed this new list *because* he thought a new language was needed. But, it is my hypothesis that Peirce may very well have given us a tool which would allow us to search for a new language.

3. THE EVOLUTION OF PEIRCE'S PERCEPTION OF THE CATEGORIES

3.1 Overview

Peirce was a complex thinker. His interest extended over a vast range of topics: he did pioneering work in the fields of logic and mathematics; he was a trained chemist; and keenly followed the developments in biology and physics. The one book that was published during his life time was a book in astronomy. He was as interested in the history of science as he was interested in the history of philosophy. He boasted of knowing a good part of Kant's first *Critique* by heart. Moreover, he was interested in practical and ethical issues, and he contributed to the theory of probability. He even offered a sort of proof for the reality of God (for God is real although he does not exist). He was also a restless thinker: ever rewriting drafts for books he never finished, never afraid of shifting position when he thought he must abandon unsatisfactory answers. This restlessness, combined with the well known fact that the *Collected Papers* were published without hardly any regard for chronology, makes it sometimes difficult to ascertain not only what the position of Peirce was at any given time, but also to determine the relationship between a particular topic and the larger problem he was trying to come to grips with. Given the paramount importance of his doctrine of categories, there ought to be something like a golden precept for Peircean scholarship: every discussion of any problem discussed by Peirce should take into account his theory of categories at a particular stage of his development. Indeed, one might even say that there is no Peircean doctrine of categories, but there is always a Peircean doctrine of categories at a particular stage of his development.

In my discussion of the evolution of his doctrine I shall make a distinction between four or five different phases: the phase of The New List of Categories (1867), the phase of the Anti-Cartesian and Pragmatic Papers, the Psychological Period, the Cosmological Period, and the Phaneroscopic Period.

3.2 The Function of Categories

The shift in his doctrine regarding the categories is already apparent from the shift in his conception of the *function* of the categories. Without dwelling on the subject, I thought the following list of expressions which describe the function of the categories may be enlightening.

(1)   Kantian conception: categories are conceptions the validity of which "consists in its impossibility of reducing the content of consciousness to unity without the introduction of it" (CP 1.545 [1867]).

(2)   Categories are thoughts about thoughts (CP 5.294 [1868]).

(3)   Categories are principles of logic, "very broad and consequently indefinite that they are hard to seize and may easily be overlooked" (CP 6.32 [1891]).

(4)   Categories are "the three elementary conceptions of metaphysics" (CP 3.422 [1892]).

(5)   Categories are "philosophical arrangements" (from Harris) (CP 1.300 [1894]).

(6)   Categories are the "forms of experience" (CP 1.452 [1896]).

(7)   Categories are the elements of "experience ... the cognitive resultant of our past lives" (CP 2.84 [1902a]).

(8)   Categories give an "account of the universe with the fewest and simplest possible categories" (CP 5.78 [1903b]).

Clearly, he begins with a logical conception of the categories, and ends with what may be called an ontological conception.

3.3 The Broadest and Simplest Statement

The table (Table 1) shows that, while the terms given under Firstness and Thirdness remain relatively stable, there is a marked development when it comes to Secondness, which at first is seen as a purely logical category, while at the end it receives an unabashedly ontological content. But before entering into the question of the development of the categories, it may be good to begin by giving a simple and straightforward description offered by Peirce himself, so that at least we know what we are talking about. It was written in 1891 as part of a text on logic:

> First is the conception of being ... independent of anything else. Second is the conception of being relative to ... something else. Third is the conception of mediation, whereby a first and second are brought into relation. (CP 6.32 [1891])

3.4 The Importance of Trinitarianism

It is always difficult to ascertain with absolute certainty where a particular insight of a thinker originates. But it is plausible that his first wife, Harriet Melusina Fay, had some influence (Fisch [1982; xxxii]). As a good unitarian, Peirce had been raised with the belief that God is one. His beloved, however, was the daughter of an Episcopalian bishop and she introduced him to the charm of Trinitarianism: the idea that God had a Son and that the relationship between Father and Son was mediated by the Spirit. But let us not speculate on the importance of this amorous influence and turn to the development of the doctrine.

3.5 The Development of the Theory of Categories

3.5.1 The First Statement: On a New List of Categories

The text: 'On a New List of Categories', is the outcome of a long process of thinking through some basic issues regarding the way we think in general, and the way in which we acquire knowledge. Apart from the question of the categories, there are at least two other themes that are related to the problem

	Firstness	Secondness	Thirdness
	Firstness	Secondness	Thirdness
1867	quality	relation	representation
1891	first	second	third
	spontaneity	dependence	mediation
	mind	matter	evolution
	chance	law	tendency to take habits
	sporting	heredity	fixation of character
	feeling	reaction	mediation
	spontaneity	dependence	mediation
1896	quality	fact	law
1897	ideas of feelings	acts of reaction	habits
	quality	shock/vividness	
	feeling	reaction	thought
1898	quality	reaction	mediation
	first qualities/ ideas	existence/reaction	potentiality/continuity
	feelings	existence	
	chance/freedom	self-willedness	continuum
	spontaneity	thing	
		insistency	
1902	orience (originality)	struggle	
1903	presentness	action	law
	quality of feeling	struggle	general
	quality of feeling	reaction	representation
	quality of feeling	mechanical force	mediation
		actuality of event	generality

Table 1: the development of Peirce's nomenclature of categories

of the categories. These I will leave out of my discussion, partly because there is no time for it, and partly because those topics will be central to some other papers given in this volume. The first is that all thought is of the nature of signs. The second is related to Peirce's major problem with Kant which led him to the view that there are three modes of reasoning which cannot be reduced one to the other: deduction, induction, and abduction.

His study of Kant's deduction of the categories led Peirce to ask the question: Given *what is*, in its most undetermined form, what are the necessary conditions for arriving at a conception of determinate Being, i.e. substance (CP 1.545 [1867])? His answer is that three such conceptions are required: quality, relation and representation. The most important aspect of these three conceptions is that there is an asymmetrical relation of dependence between them. While relation requires *relata*, the *relata* do not necessarily require a relation. Similarly, while representation requires relations and therefore *relata*, relations as such do not require representation.

On the other hand, *relata* as such are nothing but possibles without a relation connecting them, while relations as such do not mean anything (and thus are not really relations) without a representation in virtue of which they have meaning. The important insight of Peirce is that those three categories, while involving each other, are, nonetheless, irreducible one to the other.

3.5.2 The Categories and the Pragmatic Context

It has taken roughly twenty-five centuries for us to slowly apprehend that the 'original sin' of Greek thought was the separation of thought from action. The discovery of this in Peirce's mind took exactly ten years, the span which separates the still basically Kantian perspective (which dominates the text of his New List) from his pragmatic papers.

Most probably, the change must have taken Peirce almost by surprise. And though he was unmistakably the first to formulate the pragmatic maxim, he freely admitted that he had derived the basic insight of pragmatism while attending the meetings of what had been named, rather ironically, the Metaphysical Club. It was there that he learned that a belief is basically the expression of a habit, and that a habit is the expression of a readiness to act. This simple insight raises the question how beliefs come to be. How do habits evolve? And more specifically: How do those habits evolve which find their expression in our *general* beliefs?

The pragmatic theory as such does not interest us right now. But the insight that thought is meaningless unless the concepts we use can be translated into terms that are relevant to action, proved to be a decisive turn in the development of Peirce. Theories must be relevant to the way we act. If they are not, they mean nothing at all.

The relevance of this discovery for the doctrine of categories is that Peirce, although Hegelian in temperament, always insisted that there can be no generality of thought except within the context of concrete brutal events. But it was by virtue of his Hegelian temperament, that he never forgave his fellow pragmatists for confusing the expression 'relevant to action', with the expression 'for the sake of action'. It was on that account that he would finally give his own doctrine the intentionally ugly name of pragmaticism.

The topic of the categories does not as such make up part of his pragmatic doctrine. Indeed, there is some indication that he lost interest in the topic. He uses the term 'category' in the loose sense, as synonym with 'class'. On the other hand, some texts written in the same period attest to the fact that he did think in terms of the distinction between first, second and third. Thus he described 'the thread of life' as a third while the fate that snips it, as a second. Similarly, he observed that action is second, but conduct (which is action according to a law or a habit) is third (CP 1.337 [1875]).

This discrepancy may suggest that the earlier logical theory of categories and the later broader theory of first, second and third were not immediately linked to each other.

3.5.3 The Logic of Relations

Peirce was fond of reminding us that, in his words, metaphysics is the ape of logic. By this he meant to indicate that every decisive turn in the history of metaphysics is preceded by an advance in logical insight. This principle certainly applied to the development of his own doctrine of categories.

In his technical work on the Logic of Relations he treated the problem of relations in a purely formal sense. A glimpse of this formal approach is offered by the following description of dyadic and triadic relations:

> A dual relative term, such as "lover" or "servant," is a sort
> of blank form, where there are two places left blank ... But
> a triple relative term such as "giver" has two correlates,
> and is thus a blank form with three places left blank ...
> and from that we can go on in a similar way to any higher
> number. (CP 1.363 [1890])

The result of this work in logic was the insight that, while dyadic relations cannot be reduced to pairs of monadic relations and triadic relations cannot be reduced to pairs of dyadic relations, it is also true that any relationship involving more than three *relata* can always be analyzed in terms of triadic relations. And although he did not explicitly speak of a doctrine of *categories* in his technical work, clearly it was that work which finally made him see that a theory of monadic, dyadic and triadic relations was the key not only to understanding our thinking, but to our understanding of the world.

3.5.4 The Psychological Context

When, in 1879, Peirce went to the Johns Hopkins University in Baltimore to teach logic, he became acquainted with experimental psychology, a discipline which had just crossed the Atlantic from Germany. This research pertained to the phenomenon of perception. Peirce, whose official job was to be a scientist in service of the 'Survey', the Government Office charged with gathering information regarding the physical structure of the country, was fascinated by the problem of measurement, and more particularly by the philosophical problem of the status of errors of measurement. Were they the result of human limitations of perception, or was the difference in values obtained during measurement due to the behavior of things themselves? He always would favor the latter position. This is of primary importance for the understanding of his conception of Firstness. In every measurement there is an irreducible and unpredictable element which explains why every measurement yields a slightly different value.

Not only was he interested in experimental psychology. He also actively participated in the actual research and was always eager to use the knowledge obtained during those years to back up his philosophical positions.

More importantly, however, he came to clearly see the distinction between the experience of feeling or sensation, and perception. While sensation or feeling - the element of Firstness - cannot be dissociated from the quality-felt, perception - the element of Secondness - on the contrary, explicitly involves the duality of the perceiver and the perceived.

Peirce's view of sensation is probably one of the most contentious issues of his doctrine, partly because it involves a reference to an experience which cannot be expressed in words. Peirce repeatedly pointed out this difficulty, and, therefore, resorted to examples which immediately appeal to our experience. His two favorite examples were color and pain. In my experience of a particular color, there are three distinct moments. The easiest of these to understand is obviously the one which we express in a proposition: 'This is red'; meaning that what we perceive may be subsumed under the concept of the general conception of the color 'red'. And since the proposition in some way expresses what I have perceived, it expresses the duality consisting of me-perceiving-the-color or the color-perceived-by-me. These two cannot be said to be two faces of one and the same coin, for in some way the duality was *brought about*. At first, I did not perceive the color, and now the color forced itself upon me. In sensation, however, there is no duality whatever.

I am fully aware that Peirce was not the first to point out this distinction. What is original, and perhaps contentious, was the way in which he saw the difference. There are two aspects to his view. On the one hand, there is his insistence on the aspect of the radical novelty of sensation. This color 'red' is first in the sense that it is not related to anything at all, not to my consciousness, not to some electro-magnetic radiation, nor even to any other red that has ever been or will ever be felt. Peirce is not denying that when my perception or my judgment of this color is at stake, the experience is definitely made possible by my consciousness or by electro-magnetic radiation. But neither my consciousness nor the electro-magnetic energy are part of the sensation of 'red' as sensation.

Sometimes Peirce tried to point out the radical unrelatedness of a sensation by suggesting that it is possible to imagine the universe as being this 'red' and nothing else. In this respect, the example of pain may help. I have never given birth myself, but I can imagine that to a woman giving birth there is a moment in which the entire universe is pain, a moment in which there is no place for the distinction between herself and the pain she feels. Maybe the moment is very short, and even then, it *is* that moment only by virtue of the subsequent perception of pain. In fact there may be moments where the pain is so totally encompassing that the possibility of consciousness is taken away. We literally lose consciousness, and do not 'recall' the pain. In that case we cannot even say that there was *actual* pain. And, thus, Peirce insists that sensation is a mere *possible*. It is most definitely *real*, but it is real without being actual. Indeed, it is precisely what is actualized in the event which is constituted by the interaction of the quality felt and the perceiver. The total absence of duality explains that there can not be any difference between quality and feeling. 'Red' is not first a quality which is then felt, nor is it something abstracted from some process within the mind that we call a feeling. The feeling and the quality of 'red' are one and the same.

Thus, the three categories may be described as categories of consciousness. These are respectively: feelings, perceptions and thoughts. As we have seen, thought is of the nature of a habit. And the structure of habit is inherently conditional. Our habit of shaking hands is expressed in the conditional proposition: If a situation arises in which I meet a person to whom I am introduced, or whom I know but haven't seen for a while, then I shake his hand. This conditional nature of habits makes them generals, and, therefore, possibles, albeit in a different sense from the possibles which are sensations. The history of a person may be reconstructed in terms of the three categories of consciousness. We become persons as our habits grow, and those habits are symbolized in our thoughts. Those habits or thoughts arise from our perceptions which in turn are made possible by feelings or sensations.

To Peirce, the most important thing in all this was that it is impossible to describe an experience in terms of first and second only:

> First and second, agent and patient, yes and no, are
> categories which enable us roughly to describe the facts of
> experience, and they satisfy the mind for a very long time.
> But at last they are found inadequate, and the third is the
> conception which is then called for. (CP1.359 [1890])

More generally, he described the three categories of consciousness as
follows:

> ... first, feeling, the consciousness which can be included
> with an instant of time, passive consciousness of quality,
> without recognition or analysis; second, consciousness of
> an interruption into the field of consciousness, sense of
> resistance, of an external fact, of another something; third,
> synthetic consciousness, binding time together, sense of
> learning, thought. (CP 1.377 [1885])

This will still be his position at the end of his life, when explaining his three
categories to Lady Welby. The only significant difference was his emphasis
upon the fact that signs (the primary topic of their correspondence) are
linked to Thirdness (CP 8.327-32 [1904]).

3.5.5 Categories and Evolution

It would not take Peirce long before seeing that his analysis of the growth
of thought was but a particular instance of the process of growth of the
universe itself. The catalyst that brought about this generalization of
perspective was the appearance of the most spectacular and challenging
doctrine that marked the second half of the nineteenth century: the theory
of evolution.

Peirce's cosmological texts are a strange blend of an analysis of prevailing
interpretations of the theory of evolution, a polemic tirade against
mechanists and an unashamed apology for the Johannine message that the
world must be seen as the work of ever and continuously expanding love.
No wonder, Peirceans treat those texts as things we better not talk about.
But if one takes away the rhetoric, what remains is a fairly straight forward
attempt at showing that evolution is best explained in terms of the three
Categories. The laws of nature are seen as cosmic habits, some of which
have gradually evolved into increasingly hard rules as is most clearly seen
in the realm of what we usually call inorganic matter. These habits came
about as the result of interactions between unrelated qualities (CP 1.412
[1890]), which gradually and incidentally would interact, thus creating the
opportunity for associations to be formed. Thus, the universe evolves
between two virtual poles: at the beginning a world of mere and, thus,

possible qualities or feelings, at the end a world dominated by asymptotically hardening and harmonizing general rules.

For the topic of this paper, the details of this world view are less important than what the theory means for the doctrine of the categories. Whereas, originally the doctrine of the categories had been formulated within the context of purely logical considerations, Peirce would eventually come to see logic itself as the outcome of a cosmic process. Indeed, he did not hesitate to show that our three basic forms of logical argument - deduction, induction and abduction (the reasoning of which the conclusion is a hypothesis further to be tested) - are simply the expression of our physiological hardware which has grown from the evolutionary process.

Peirce considered his cosmological theory a philosophical hypothesis which, like any other scientific hypothesis, derived its meaning from the possibility of empirically testing it. And he even went as far as saying that he had found the empirical evidence, although to my knowledge, he never put the evidence on the table.

3.5.6 The Cenopythagorean Categories

When Peirce had left the 'Survey' and was, to all intents and purposes, a man without a job, he wanted to finally put order into his philosophical and logical thought. It was his intention to produce encyclopedic works in which the various aspects of his thought would be integrated. One problem which had always interested him would now become of paramount importance. It was the problem which his great example, Hegel, had faced when writing his *Encyclopedia:* the question of the exact relationship between the various sciences. And, like Hegel, Peirce also thought that a thorough study of the architectonic of science required an exhaustive study of the categories, because they are the necessary condition of any thought whatsoever.

But, while Hegel's theory of category constituted his logic, Peirce had become convinced that even logic (in any approbation of the term) presupposed something more basic. Any science, even formal science, presupposes an analysis of the basic constituents of all appearance. These are: the brutal fact of the appearance itself (Secondness), the novel constituents of appearance (Firstness), and an element in virtue of which the appearance has meaning (Thirdness). Because the business of charting those three elements is not a science properly speaking (since it makes science possible), Peirce favored the term *Phaneroscopy* or *Ideoscopy* over *Phenomenology*. This was in order to emphasize that anyone who *looks* at what appears, should be able to observe those elements, independently of saying (and that is what a -logy implies) what they are or how they function. Such Phaneroscopy reveals what Peirce was to call the Cenopythagorean Categories. He calls them *Pythagorean* because they are expressed in terms of numbers, and they are *ceno*-Pythagorean because they are common (**koinos**) to all that appears. The business of such Phaneroscopy is:

> ... to unravel the tangled skein [of] all that in any sense appears and wind it into distinct forms; or in other words, to make the ultimate analysis of all experiences the first task to which philosophy has to apply itself. (CP 1.280 [1902b])

And one year later, he wrote how such analysis is to be done:

> ... what we have to do, as students of phenomenology, is simply to open our mental eyes and look well at the phenomenon and say what are the characteristics that are never wanting in it, whether that phenomenon be something that outward experience forces upon our attention, or whether it be the wildest of dreams, or whether it be the most abstract and general of the conclusions of science. (CP 5.41 [1903a])

Not only did Peirce explicitly say that Phaneroscopy is not logic, but he also insisted that it is not metaphysics.

Moreover, it would be misleading to stress the resemblance between his Phaneroscopy and Husserl's *Phenomenology*. From the very beginning, Husserl's *Phenomenology* was framed within a perspective of consciousness. It seems that, in his later views on the categories, Peirce regarded consciousness as a rather uninteresting accidental aspect of what is going on. Thus, in 1897 he wrote:

> Consciousness may mean any one of the three categories. But if it is to mean Thought it is more without us than within. It is we that are in it, rather than it in any of us. (CP 8.256 [1897])

In one such exposition of the categories (as elements of appearance) he pointed out the characteristics of the three basic elements of appearance: qualities are "somewhat vague and potential", they "are concerned in facts but they do not make up facts", they "do not resist or react". Occurrence on the other hand is perfectly individual, it happens here and now, it involves resistance; while the third element is the element of laws or thoughts (CP 1.419-20 [1896]).

3.5.7 Metaphysical Conception of the Categories

In the end, it is not always clear whether Peirce still made a real distinction between the categories in the phaneroscopic sense and the categories in the metaphysical sense. Or, one might say, if there is a difference, it certainly is a difference that *makes* no difference. In other words, it is a meaningless difference. For instance, at one point he wrote:

> Such, at least, is the doctrine I have been teaching for twenty-five years, and which, if deeply pondered, will be found to enwrap an entire philosophy ... Nature only appears intelligible so far as it appears rational, that is, so far as its processes are seen to be like processes of thought ... I will only mention here that the ideas which belong to the three forms of rhemata are firstness, secondness, thirdness; firstness, or spontaneity; secondness, or dependence; thirdness, or mediation. (CP 3.422 [1892])

Clearly, he thought that the elements of appearance coincided with the elements of Nature. There is a lot more to be said about the categories. However, it is not my intention to give an exhaustive analysis of Peirce's doctrine. The main point is, in Peirce's own words:

> But what I mean is, that all that there is, is First, Feelings; Second, Efforts; Third, Habits. (CP 6.201 [1898])

4. THE CENTRAL PLACE OF SECONDNESS

There is no doubt that Peirce's Thirdness was the most important category. In this he was quite explicitly Hegelian: "Reality is an affair of Thirdness as Thirdness, that is, in its mediation between Secondness and Firstness" (CP 5.121 [1903c]).

But Peirce was equally anti-Hegelian in his insistence on Secondness as the condition for actual being:

> For as long as things do not act upon one another there is no sense or meaning in saying that they have any being, unless it be that they are such in themselves that they may perhaps come into relation with others. (CP 1.25 [1903d])

Secondness, defined abstractly, is any sort of dual relationship. But the evidence is overwhelming that, when Peirce thought of Secondness, it was always in terms of effort, volition, reaction, struggle or, more generally, occurrence:

> We find secondness in occurrence, because an occurrence
> is something whose existence consists in our knocking up
> against it. A hard fact is of the same sort; that is to say, it
> is something which is there, and which I cannot think
> away, but am forced to acknowledge as an object or
> second beside myself, the subject or number one, and
> which forms material for the exercise of my will. (CP
> 2.358 [1890])

If the categories are elements of appearance, then there must be an
appearing. And appearing is an occurrence. And thus, although it may be
that the *definiteness* of appearance is a matter of Thirdness, such Thirdness
can only *be* in respect to the element of Secondness.

5. THE CATEGORIES IN A NUTSHELL

If it is correct to say that Peirce moved from the conviction that categories
are merely a question of logic, to the conviction that logic is itself the
expression of an ongoing evolutionary process; and if it is correct to say that
such evolution is an evolution of occurrences, of reaction, of struggle, etc.,
then we might propose the following interpretation of a Peircean doctrine of
the categories:

(1)   There is what I now shall call the Peircean Ontological
Principle: If there is no Secondness, there is nothing at all.
Indeed, Thirdness is of the nature of thought, of law, of
meaning, and all such concepts are related to habit-forming; but all habit-forming presupposes that there be
occurrences which may be suitable to habit-forming. That
does not mean that there is first Secondness and then
Thirdness. Any such expressions are misrepresentations,
for all three categories are always necessary elements of
appearance.
Similarly, when it comes to Firstness which is the element
of originality, of independence, etc., such Firstness is in
and by itself merely possible in the precise sense that it
has no actuality apart from the occurrence in virtue of
which there is appearance.

(2)   Any occurrence owes its *content* to Firstness, but owes its
definiteness, its form to Thirdness which is of the nature
of habit.

(3)   By virtue of its definiteness, an occurrence signifies and,
therefore, has the function of a sign of which the meaning
(the interpretant) is of the nature of Thirdness.

(4)   An occurrence without meaning literally means nothing at all; and, thus, in a very real sense, it does not *occur* at all.

(5)   A law, a thought (not in the sense of *cogitatio*, but in the sense of *cogitatum*), a meaning, that is not in any way relevant to an occurrence is an empty thought. But in as much as such thought does occur, in as much as it is a *cogitatio* which consists in proposing an empty thought, it may have great influence.

The question now presents itself to us: So what? For the Peirceans among us, 'so what' means: What is the pragmatic meaning of this doctrine of categories? In what sense is it relevant to what we do? Does it *make* any difference? To non-Peirceans, the question is: Why should we attach any importance to this at all? In what sense is the 'New List' of Peirce superior to Aristotle's or Kant's list of categories?

6. INFORMATION AND THE CATEGORIES

In a telling passage, Peirce chastises Hegel's followers for not having treated their master right. Had they done so, they would have done what any true philosopher would wish his disciples to do: "to reform their master's system, and to render his statement of it obsolete" (CP 1.524 [1903d]).

I don't know whether I am worthy of considering myself Peirce's disciple. But should I be, then I should heed his advice and render not his system, but *the statement* of his system obsolete. Not for the sake of showing he is wrong, but because the problems we face demand it. At the beginning of my paper I have suggested that the real problems facing us are related to the problem that the language we speak is no longer fit to express what it is we want to say. Let me quote once more the neurobiologist doing research on the riddle of our memory:

> The self is not a little person inside the brain. It is a perpetually recreated neurobiological state, so continuously and consistently reconstructed that the owner never knows it is being remade.

When reading a passage like this, we can do one of two things: laugh and say that here is again a statement of a mad scientist who is yet to discover that a person is a subject endowed with a mind, etc., etc.; or, we can take him seriously and tell him that the way of stating his position is interesting, but that it unfortunately cannot be expressed in the language he uses. He literally needs new tools. The Whiteheadians among us would, I submit, probably say that the neurobiologist is saying something which is very Whiteheadian in tone. And certainly Whitehead built a very strong case for the necessity of a new language, and, therefore, for a *new list of categories*.

But I would like to suggest that the missing link between the language of the neurobiologist and the metaphysics of Whitehead is a concept which allows us to link the two. And I submit that there is such a concept. It is a concept which somehow has infiltrated itself into our thought without us noticing it, almost *in spite of* the language we speak.

I mean the concept of 'information'. Here is a concept which is ubiquitously present. Yet, there are only a few philosophers who deem it worthy of even a single comment. It is not easy to say what we mean by information. I would submit that its use may be divided into three sorts of interpretation: information in the *technical sense* which is involved in Shannon's concept of the quantity of information, of which the unit is the binary unit or the 'bit'; information in the *epistemological sense* as that from which we derive knowledge; and information in the *ontological sense* of being the sort of stuff of which we say that, for instance, it is 'stored' in our genes.

The link between those three usages may well be related to the way in which engineers often speak when they say that information is whatever makes a difference. In fact that comes close to the original intention of the word: *informatio* is an activity whereby form arises. In other words, one might define information as an informative *event*. And, if so, the distinction immediately imposes itself between the fact *that* the event takes place and, thus, makes a difference and the kind of difference the event makes. We have here exactly the distinction between the aspect of Secondness and the aspect of Thirdness. And since there is no event without the duality which relates what makes a difference to the difference made, there is also the element of Firstness. In other words, information is the one concept that perfectly fits the specifications of Peirce's categories.

Elsewhere I have argued why information may very well be the concept that is so basic that it may be a good candidate to replace the worn out concept of Being. I was delighted to see that even among theoretical physicists there are voices suggesting that information is a concept more basic than energy or mass. The question is whether we are ready to abandon not only the myth that there is in our brain a little person, but also the myth that we are things, and are surrounded by other thing-like entities. The old bags are showing signs of wear and tear.

If the suggestion that Peirce's categories demand a genuinely new language is correct, and if the suggestion that the key-concept of such language is the concept of information, then it is more urgent than ever that we take Peirce seriously.

References

FISCH, M. [1982] 'Introduction', in: M.H. Fisch *et al.* (eds.) ***Writings of Charles S. Peirce: A Chronological Edition.*** *Vol.1*, Bloomington, IN: Indiana University Press.

GEARY, J. [1997] 'A Trip Down Memory's Lanes', in: *TIME*, May 5th. The quote is provided by neurobiologist Antonio Damasio.

PEIRCE, C.S. [1867] 'On a New List of Categories. Proceedings of the American Academy of Arts and Sciences 7'.

PEIRCE, C.S. [1868] 'Some Consequences of Four Incapacities [claimed for Man]', in: *Journal of Speculative Philosophy* 1868-1869.

PEIRCE, C.S. [1875] 'Third', an unpublished fragment.

PEIRCE, C.S. [1885] 'One, Two, Three: Fundamental Categories of Thought and of Nature', unpublished.

PEIRCE, C.S. [1890] 'A Guess at the Riddle', unpublished.

PEIRCE, C.S. [1891] 'The Architecture of Theories', *The Monist* 2: 161-176.

PEIRCE, C.S. [1892] 'The Critic of Arguments', second of two published papers in: *The Open Court*.

PEIRCE, C.S. [1894] 'The List of Categories: A Second Essay', unpublished.

PEIRCE, C.S. [1896] 'The Logic of Mathematics: An Attempt to Develop My Categories from Within', unpublished.

PEIRCE, C.S. [1897] Letter to William James.

PEIRCE, C.S. [1898] 'The Logic of Continuity', draft of eighth lecture of the Cambridge lectures: 'On Reasoning and the Logic of Things', delivered in 1898.

PEIRCE, C.S. [1902a] 'Intended Characters of this Treatise', in: *Minute Logic*, Ch. 2, unpublished.

PEIRCE, C.S. [1902b] 'Classification of the Sciences', in: *Minute Logic*, Ch. I, Prelogical Notions, Section 1, unpublished.

PEIRCE, C.S. [1903a] 'On Phenomenology', draft of the second lecture of a series of lectures on pragmatism, delivered at Harvard University in 1903.

PEIRCE, C.S. [1903b] 'On the Categories', draft of the third lecture of a series of lectures on pragmatism, delivered at Harvard University in 1903.

PEIRCE, C.S. [1903c] 'On Three Kinds of Goodness', draft of the fifth lecture of a series of lectures on pragmatism, delivered at Harvard University in 1903.

PEIRCE, C.S. [1903d] 'The Three Universal Categories and their Utility', draft of the third lecture of a series of lectures on pragmatism, delivered at Harvard University in 1903.

PEIRCE, C.S. [1904] Letter to Lady Welby.

PEIRCE'S NATURAL KINDS

JAAP VAN BRAKEL

1. A STATE OF CONFUSION

Opinions differ widely as to what typical examples of natural kinds would be. In two publications that reverberated through the philosophy of science, mind and language, Kripke [1980] and Putnam [1975] made gold, water and tiger famous as natural kinds. Putnam also proposed horses, electricity and multiple sclerosis as natural kinds. Kripke mentioned yellow. In an important article on natural kinds by Quine [1969], the primary example is red. But, according to Hacking [1991], colors are not natural kinds, potential candidates being: "all sorts of animals, vegetables, minerals, insects and fish" as well as 'stone' and 'stomach'. He is sceptical about Putnam's electricity and multiple sclerosis and thinks that social kinds (people, their behavior and creations) should be kept apart from natural kinds. Boyd [1991] however, arguing against Hacking [1991], claims most social kinds are natural kinds.[1] According to Boyd, any kind that functions in induction or explanation has a claim to be a natural kind.

Perhaps the latter comes closest to Peirce's view. Peirce considers (at some point or other in his career), as examples of natural classes: chemical elements, chemical compounds, all animals and plants, the sciences (ordered hierarchically), stoves, lamps (classified according to purpose), artists, business men, scientists, and classifications of works of art according to nature of composition (Hulswit [1997]). Other less common proposals for natural kinds include: dreams, good stories, well-formed arguments and illocutionary forces.[2] Discussions rage as to whether 'person', 'belief' or 'disease' is or is not a natural kind.[3]

Returning to Hacking's list of natural kinds, Wilkerson [1988] disputes giving 'vegetable' or 'stone' the status of natural kind; such entities afford superficial knowledge, not detailed scientific analysis. Wilkerson [1988] argues that biological kinds are prototypical natural kinds. In contrast, Dupré [1989] pointed out that Wilkerson's examples, do not name *scientific* kinds, i.e. biological species or higher taxa; neither 'wolves' nor 'oaks',

---

1. See also on social kinds: Currie [1988], Wilkerson [1995; ch. 3].

2. Bruner [1986; 11], Flanagan [1995], Searle and Vanderveken [1985; 179].

3. See on belief: Needham [1972], Ramsey *et al.* [1991; 207,281]; on person: Clark [1991], Lowe [1991], Rovane [1993]; on disease: D'Amico [1995].

Wilkerson's examples, correspond with a biological species or higher or lower taxa.

Moreover, the majority of philosophers of biology deny that species are natural *kinds*; instead they would be historical *individuals*.[4] In a later publication Wilkerson changed his view:[5]

> Biological natural kinds are determined by genetic real essences which are causally responsible for the behaviour of individual members of the kind. But, since there is considerable interspecific genetic similarity and intraspecific genetic variation, there are far more biological natural kinds than species. (Wilkerson [1995; 133])

Finally, concerning the received view that water, gold, and tiger are prototypical natural kinds, Churchland [1989; 295] argues that these are merely *practical* kinds. As "genuine natural kinds" he lists "mass, length, duration, charge, color, energy, momentum" (where 'color' refers to the colors of quarks).

2. DEFINITIONS OF NATURAL KINDS

That there is no agreement on examples is understandable given that there is little consensus on the definition of natural kind. Some writers define natural kinds with reference to essences or having 'genuine' or essential properties; others make the connection with natural necessities or true and explanatory laws of nature; again others put the emphasis on the causal features of the world or on the explanatory role of natural kinds or their involvement in inductions.

There seems to be some sort of consensus that natural kind, law, cause, induction, explanation, disposition, and a few others, are syncategorematic terms, and part of these connections are often included in definitions of natural kinds.[6] For example, in the glossary of an anthology natural kind is defined as:

> A type of property, process, state, event, or object studied by science, mentioned in scientific laws, and assumed to be a causal feature of the world. The primary instances of

---

4. See Ereshefsky [1991], Ghiselin [1987], Kluge [1990], Splitter [1988], Williams [1985].

5. Confer Dupré [1993].

6. See for example: Bigelow [1990], Bigelow *et al.* [(1992], Boyd [1989, 1991], De Sousa [1984], Griffiths [1996], Johnson [1990], Kitcher [1984], Lowe [1991], Millikan [1984].

natural kinds are objects of scientific taxonomy, such as
electrons in physics, zinc in chemistry, and species in
biology. Natural kinds are contrasted with phenomena that
are assigned no such systematic, organising role, such as
an event's occurring after I drop this pen, or an object's
being located 34 miles west of the Liberty Bell. (Boyd *et
al.* [1991; 778f])

But, as one might expect, there is no consensus on the meaning of terms
like 'law' or 'explanation'; so it doesn't bring us nearer to *the* definition of
natural kind. Moreover, there is also an inclination to avoid difficult
questions. For example,[7] Horgan [1982; 36] says: "Providing an adequate
philosophical account of natural kinds is no trivial task, of course, but I shall
leave that task to one side here"; and Currie [1990; 246]: "Of course I'm in
no good position to say exactly what it takes for a property to be natural,
though I assume that by and large we can agree on particular cases"; and,
finally, Hirsch [1982; 252]: "The notion of a natural kind is surely
problematical. I want, however, to take this notion pretty much for granted
in the present discussion".

3. PEIRCE'S DEFINITION OF NATURAL KIND

Hence, there is no consensus among philosophers of how to characterize
natural kinds (as distinct from artificial, nominalistic, or other kinds of non-
natural kinds) - the problem being of course that they don't agree on the
reference or sense of 'natural' or in their general epistemological and
metaphysical approach to the natural world. Let us now look at what Peirce
has to say on natural kinds or, what I will take to be the same, 'real kinds'
or 'natural classes'.[8]

In his 1901 article 'Kind', in Baldwin's *Dictionary of Philosophy and
Psychology*, Peirce says:

Any class which, in addition to its defining character, has
another that is of permanent interest and is common and
peculiar to its members, is destined to be conserved in that
ultimate conception of the universe at which we aim, and
is accordingly to be called "real". (CP 6.384)

---

7. Similar comments can be found in Oddie [1991], Pargetter [1988], and Savellos [1992].

8. My paper is as much about natural kinds as about Peirce. The phrase 'natural kinds' in
the title refers as much to Peirce's examples as to his philosophical arguments. For an account
of the embeddedness of natural classes in his philosophy see Hulswit [1997]. Another important
paper on Peirce's natural kinds is Haack [1992].

On various other occasions Peirce gives definitions of real kinds or natural classes; but, with the exception of the relation of natural kinds to final causes, made later by Peirce, the definition just quoted is representative of his views.[9]

The two themes I want to address are: first, which kinds, if any, are excluded from Peirce's definition of real classes? Second, does Peirce's view that the man of science accounts for every property in terms of "a small number of primary characters" (CP 6.384), imply eliminativism?[10]

In his 1901 article just quoted, Peirce presents what has been described as a devastating critique of Mill's theory of natural kinds. Mill had said: "White things are not distinguished by any common properties, except whiteness: or if they are, it is only by such as are in some way connected with whiteness" (Mill [1843; 122]). Peirce points out that Mill must assume that our interests determine those properties. Were that assumption not made, it would not be true that white things only share a small number of properties. Moreover, it is the purpose of science to find out about the relation between properties of natural kinds. Hence, that the properties of white things are "in some way connected with whiteness" is no argument against 'white things' being a natural kind. However, some of Peirce's own examples seem to be open to the same objection. For example, he suggests that "animals having legs do not form a natural group; for they are not

---

9. Confer: "Real kinds [are] classes which differ from all others in more respects than one" (W 1: 287 [1865]); "[A natural class is a class that] has other properties than those which are implied in its definition" (W 1: 418 [1866]); "Every class which embodies information, in the sense that something is true of all its members beyond what is involved in the definition of the class, is a natural class" (NEM 4: 15 [1902]). And after Peirce made the connection with final causes (Hulswit [1997]): "[A natural class is a class] of which all the members owe their existence to a common final cause" (CP 1.204 [1902]); "[A natural class is] a class the existence of whose members is due to a common and peculiar final cause" (CP 1.211 [1902]).

10. Eliminativism in the narrow sense is the view in the philosophy of mind that "the thesis that our commonsense conception of psychological phenomena constitutes a radically false theory, a theory so fundamentally defective that both the principles and the ontology of that theory will eventually be displaced, rather than smoothly reduced, by completed neuroscience" (Churchland [1989; 1]). In the wider sense it is a form of eliminative reductionism across the board: "The familiar multitude of putatively natural kinds embraced by common sense, and by the many derivative sciences, are at best merely practical kinds. Genuine natural kinds form a very small, aristocratic elite among kinds in general, being found only in the most basic laws of an all-embracing physics" (Churchland [1989; 295]). "My tentative ontology continues to consist of quarks and their compounds, also classes of such things, classes of such classes, and so on, pending evidence to the contrary" (Quine [1992]). This eliminativism can be pushed even further into hyperpythagoreanism, as illustrated in the following quotation of Dirac [1939]: "If we express the present epoch, 2×10^9 years, in terms of a unit of time defined by the atomic constants, we get a number of the order 10^{39}, which characterizes the present in an absolute sense. Might it not be that all present events correspond to properties of this large number, and, more generally, that the whole history of the universe corresponds to properties of the whole sequence of natural numbers?".

separated from all others in any other important particular" (CP 1.205). Perhaps Peirce is less concerned about the *number* of shared properties (which is central to his dispute with Mill) than about their *quality*. He says:

> An *important* character is obviously one upon which others depend, that is, one the inclusion of which in a definition renders true general propositions concerning the object defined possible; and the more such propositions a character renders possible, the more important it is. (W 2: 443)

But if we drop local interests, any character renders true an infinite number of general propositions concerning the object as defined (Goodman [1972], Hirsch [1993]).

Other questions that can be raised about Peirce's definition include: What is meant by 'real'? Is it the same 'real' as when he says:[11] "*Red* is relative to sight, but the fact that this or that is in that relation to vision that we call being red is not *itself* relative to sight; it is a real fact" (CP 5.430). This suggests the class of red things is also a natural class. Peirce's response to Mill would lend support for that. But Hacking said: "No one in the great tradition of natural kinds has seriously regarded the colours as natural kinds" (Hacking [1991; 115]), recently echoed by Millikan [1997], who says "a 'white thing' isn't on the scale with substances, as nothing can be learned about it". Hacking included Peirce (together with Mill and Russell) in 'the great tradition' of views on natural kinds. However, it is not clear how to understand Peirce's criticism of Mill, if white things are not accepted as a natural class. Contrary to Mill's views and those of many other writers on the subject (like Millikan [1997]), who exclude colors from natural kinds, various things can be learned about, say, white. White will always reflect most of the incident light; there is no transparent white; the reflectance of white objects (as contrasted with luminance) is the same throughout changes in illumination, and so on (Westphal [1987]).

Coming back to 'real', is it 'real' if it occurs in the ultimate conception? Does the ultimate conception determine what is of permanent interest? Is the 'same' interest applicable to all human beings? If 'real' refers to consensus at the end of inquiry, what sort of consensus is it? Is it part of the *telos* that there *is* an end of inquiry and there *will be* a consensus?

I'll start with a more specific question: Which classes and characteristics remain in the ultimate conception? Will it include colors like green or only

---

11. Confer CP 1.422 and Friedman [1995]. Whiteness is real too (CP 8.14). Elsewhere (van Brakel [1993]) I have discussed the connections between Peirce's view on natural kinds, 'generals' and his 'realism(s)'.

the color of quarks? Will the hardness of diamonds be included or only the "high polemerization of the molecule" (CP 5.457)? And what about the boiling point of water? Presumably that should stay - how could it not stay? But what then is *not* included? I'll show that if we reply 'yes' to keeping the color green in the ultimate conception, we are forced to accept a form of pluralism, which will remain till the end of inquiry. On the other hand, if we prefer not to associate Peirce's philosophy with a form of pluralism, then eliminativism is forced on us; then not only the green and red will go, but also the boiling point of water, the 'high polemerization of the molecule', water, tigers, and everything else we know about at the moment.

4. PLURALISM OR ELIMINATIVISM

One underlying problem is the question of what the right primitives are: the substances or kinds in terms of which other kinds can be analytically defined. A further problem is whether asking what the right primitives are is the right question to ask. Most writers on natural kinds would say that red square or red flag or red cow are not primitive. But why not? What would Peirce say? Apparently, Peirce takes for granted that 'red cow' is not a natural kind.[12] But why would he say that? Presumably, he appeals to a generally shared intuition. But that too is what Mill did, when claiming that white was not a natural kind.

Why would 'cow' be a natural class and 'red cow' not? What about cows and buffalos? Do they constitute two natural classes or only one? Consider too the following. African pastoral peoples distinguish many types of 'cows', referring to them with words that seem to identify them in terms of color pattern, but other unique properties are ascribed to each type. For example, the Dinka distinguish the following types of 'cow': *jak, jok, kwe, gihjak, kur, kul, bil, rol, par, rial, kwac, wea, gwong, nyal, cuor, reng, ding, kar, kwol*, and more (Evans-Pritchard [1933; 5]). Dinka will tell you, if we don't insist on literal translations, that different types of 'cows' have different final causes - hence they might all be considered different natural kinds. Moreover, a few hundred miles down the road these final causes will be different. The Bodi distinguish the following types of 'cow': *tul'ka, kordi, bilasi, eldi, ludi, gelli, coburi, koro, bolloga, pologi, cokaji, lingili-idi*, and others (Fukui [1979]).

Perhaps one is inclined to push aside these 'finer' distinctions as irrelevant to the ultimate conception. But where should one draw the line. Are Dinka 'cows', the same natural class as Bodi 'cows'? As it happens, they have a quite different *gestalt*. Probably they share enough properties to place them in one natural class. But why should we stop at *cow*? Why not

---

12. W 1: 416 [1866]; MS 421; I owe this reference to Hulswit [1997; 734].

drop cows as natural kinds, and consider only mammals, or animals as a natural kind? How would one find the middle road between the extremes of each individual being a different natural kind and the world being the only natural kind? Peirce might appeal to some underlying decisive factor, as when he predicts the invention of DNA, saying there might be "enough different kinds of protoplasm for each organ, or even cell of every individual animal or plant that ever existed on earth to have a unique kind of its own" (CP 1.261). But because of interspecies genetic similarities and intraspecies genetic variation, this helps little to find the 'natural' division between natural classes.

All writers on the subject, including Peirce, seem to make an intuitive appeal to what is obvious, what is primitive and what is complex. White, red, green, yellow, blue, black would be primitive; *lhenxa* or *grue* would not; *lhenxa* is a Kwakw'ala word, the reference of which, in standardized 'decontextualised' experiments, includes most greens and yellows; both a yellow lemon and a green apple are *lhenxa* (Saunders and van Brakel [1996]); the term *grue* applies to all things examined before *t* just in case they are green but to other things just in case they are blue.[13]

Similarly, mouse, and perhaps vulture, would be primitive, but *vovetas* not; *vovetas* is a Tsistsistas (Cheyenne) word (van Brakel [1991]), the reference of which includes most vultures (*Cathartidae*), the common nighthawk (*Chordeiles minor*), swarms of green darners (*Anax junius*, a dragonfly), swarms of red skimmers (*Libellula saturata*), and tornado's (meteorological events).[14] Clearly, *vovetas* doesn't meet the natural-kind-criterium of 'genetic similarity'; but why would the 'natural' interest be genetic similarity, and not 'whirling movements' or whatever motivates speakers of Tsistsistas to speak about *vovetas*?

In response to Goodman's *grue*, Chomsky has said that "every language learner (in fact, every mouse, chimpanzee, etc.) uses green rather than grue as a basis for generalization" (quoted in Goodman [1972; 378]). But Goodman is surely right to say that speakers accustomed to projecting 'grue' rather than 'green' would be equally confident that animals use grue rather then green as a basis for generalization.

This may sound counter-intuitive, but then using *lhenxa* or *vovetas* will also sound counter-intuitive to many who are confronted for the first time with *lhenxa* or *vovetas*.

I now want to show that Peirce's views are compatible with a form of pluralism in which the distinction between natural and non-natural classes

---

13. Goodman [1972; 381]. For discussion on 'grue' see Stalker [1994]. For many 'real-life' examples like *lhenxa* see Saunders and van Brakel [1997].

14. In the literature on 'western' natural kinds, there is no agreement as to whether events like tornado's or earthquakes are natural kinds (Savellos [1992], Wilkerson [1995; 38-52]).

disappears. I will illustrate this with color, though similar arguments work for cows or water or whatever.[15] The question is, what is going to be kept in the ultimate conception of the universe. Will only 'red' and 'green' stay or will *lhenxa* too? If so, what would their defining characteristics be? Consider the following specification of the characters of green and *lhenxa*.[16]

GREEN:

(i)   *defining characteristic*: the class **G** which is called 'green' by most speakers of English;

(ii)   *ultimate characteristic*: each element of **G** causes in 'normal' human beings a negative signal in the LM channel and no signal in the LM/S channel the absolute value of which is larger than the signal in the LM channel.

LHENXA:

(i)   *defining characteristic*: the class **L** which is called *lhenxa* by most speakers of Kwak'wala;

(ii)   *ultimate characteristic*: each element of **L** causes in 'normal' human beings a negative signal in the LM channel and a positive signal in the LM/S channel.

One response might be to say that this example strongly suggests the nature of the ultimate conception: in the ultimate conception there is no room for *either* green *or lhenxa*. What belongs in the ultimate conception is the LM-channel (or whatever is substituted in successor science). This leads straight down the primrose path of eliminativism, which in places Peirce seems to endorse. For example, the assumption of underlying essences comes across clearly in Peirce's examples from chemistry and biology.

---

15. It may be less obvious that the argument might work for chemical substances like water; but see van Brakel [1986, 1997].

16. The description of the ultimate characteristics follows the dominant theory of color perception. There are three cone types in the retina, which are maximally responsive to short (S), middle (M) and long (L) wavelengths of light, respectively. According to the dominant theory the 'information' thus reaching the cones is processed further in one achromatic and two chromatic channels. The first channel processes overall luminance and is also called the brightness channel. The second channel processes the relative intensities of the long and mid-spectral light, but it is insensitive to absolute levels of illumination - this is the LM channel (also called the red/green channel). Activity in the third channel is proportional to the difference between the activation of the S cones and the combined activation of the L and M cones - this is the LM/S channel (also called the yellow/blue channel). But this simple psychological model is at odds with many experimental results. For details on, and criticisms of this theory see Saunders and van Brakel [1997]. For the argument in the main text the technical details are irrelevant.

Diamonds, he says, share many properties, including hardness, because of the "high polemerization of the molecule" (CP 5.457). And more explicitly, in a passage from which I have already quoted: "the chemical constitution of the protoplasm [is] the sole determining cause of the forms of all animals and plants" (CP 1.261). Many authors interpret Peirce's philosophy in such a way as to imply a form of eliminativism. Most, however, are not aware of the consequences of their interpretation. Wiggins has given an excellent summary of this kind of reading of Peirce:

> Suppose we take a Peircean view of Science as discovering that which is destined, the world being what it is, to be ultimately agreed by all who investigate ... Cosmic rationality in belief will then consist in conforming one's beliefs so far as possible to the truths that are destined to survive in this process of convergence ... Seeing the world in this way, one sees no meaning in anything ... This Peircean conceptual scheme *articulates* nothing that it is humanly possible to care about. (Wiggins [1988; 152-3])

If we refuse to follow the track of eliminativism, the green/*lhenxa* example leads to a very different conclusion. Differences in the history of life forms, theoretical innovation or concept formation lead to different classifications.[17] Any serious suggestion concerning a universal, natural classification can only lead down the eliminativist path (van Brakel [1992]). This remains so through every step down to the end of inquiry. There is no way of making strict connections between classifications in the manifest life forms and those of various types of scientific and other inquiry, neatly fitting them in one ultimate reality. In brief, as to colors, both green and *lhenxa* have to stay in the ultimate conception. Both are real and cannot be reduced to one or the other (or 'the one' underlying mechanism). Each fits the descriptions Peirce gives of the ultimate opinion. Both green and *lhenxa* fulfill the requirement that:

> ... what I mean by the idea's conferring existence upon the individual members of the class is that it confers upon them the power of working out results in this world, that it confers upon them, that is to say, organic existence, or, in one word, life. (CP 1.220)

---

17. Confer: "Generality is real, but dividing things into classes reflects our interests and conventional decisions" (Hookway [1985; 249]).

5. RELATION BETWEEN SCIENCE, PHILOSOPHY AND COMMON SENSE

Although Peirce had great respect for science, emphasizing the interest free quest for truth; nevertheless, he was aware that at crucial points the results of inquiry depend on extra-scientific matters.[18]

First, there is the close connection between Peirce's metaphysics and common sense, or the manifest life forms. Peirce says the purpose of metaphysics is to investigate the most general characteristics of reality and of real objects. Metaphysical inquiry uses the same methods as science, but is part of philosophy, because its inquiry does not depend on special observations or experimental techniques; rather on ordinary everyday experience.[19] Fallibilism applies to science: science cannot reach truth in the short run, but philosophy (metaphysics) might. Metaphysical hypotheses can be tested relative to ordinary and trivial observations.

Second, Peirce explains the success of science by appealing to an instinct that allows us to formulate or choose clever hypotheses. For example he says that "there is a special adaptation of the mind to the universe, so that we are more apt to make true theories than we otherwise should be" (CP 2.749).[20] There are passages in Peirce's writings which would support interpreting the instinctive aspect of abduction as restricted to heuristics and controlled by 'rational' induction (Kapitan [1992]). But Peirce also says that "neither deduction nor induction can ever add the smallest item to the data of perception ... there is no other good class in which to put abduction but that of inferences" (HP 2: 899). Further, which theory to test is based on instinctive common-sense plausibility judgements. Such instinctive judgements do not come under 'conceptual activity'; they are *not* the result of critical thought;[21] they cannot be reduced to a mere following of rules. Hence the pragmatic principle doesn't apply to them. The most important characteristics of this instinctive judgement are "its groundlessness, its ubiquity, and its trustworthiness" (HP 2: 898; MS 692 [1901]).[22]

---

18. CP 5.521-2. Hence, these 'extra-scientific matters' better stay in the ultimate conception as well. For discussion see Rescher [1995] and Delaney [1995].

19. CP 1.34; 5.438ff; 6.3; HP 2: 825, 880.

20. Confer: "the human intellect is peculiarly adapted to the comprehension of the laws and facts of nature" (CP 2.750); "a natural instinct for truth is, after all, the sheer-anchor of science" (CP 7.220); "*instinctive insight* or genius tending to make him guess those laws aright or nearly aright" (CP 5.604); "thoughts ... naturally show a tendency to agree with the laws of nature" (MS 92 [1903-4]); "the instinctive result of human experience ought to have so vastly more weight than any scientific result" (CP 5.522); also CP 2.749-54; 5.174; 5.181; 6.418.

21. CP 5.173.

22. Confer Graybosch [1992], who refers to MS 755 where Peirce sees a continuity between common sense and science, because of two natural gifts: the capacity to understand 'folk physics' that supports survival and the capacity to understand other people's thinking.

Third, there is a dependence of the method of inquiry (both in metaphysics and science) on esthetics and ethics. There is such a thing as a *summum bonum* (the ideal of ideals),[23] which is fed by three normative sciences, viz., logic in the wide sense, ethics, and esthetics. For example, "all probable reasoning (which is part of logic) ... depends upon a moral virtue, that of sincerity" (HP 2: 833).[24] The purpose of inquiry, i.e. reasoning, comes eventually under the jurisdiction of ethics and the method of inquiry under that of esthetics.

> Esthetics, therefore, although I have terribly neglected it, appears to be possibly the first indispensable propedeutic to logic, and the logic of esthetics to be a distinct part of the science of logic that ought not to be omitted. (CP 2.199)

And there is no way to separate logic and ethics: "Logic is rooted in the social principle" (CP 2.654); "the social principle is rooted intrinsically in logic" (CP 5.354).

Hence, pragmaticism or Peirce's metaphysical cosmology explicitly includes an affective and moral dimension, inherent in such expressions as 'cheerful hope', 'love of truth', 'evolutionary love', 'Sensible Heart', and such like.[25] Here the pragmatic principle does not apply in a straightforward way. The final justification of abduction and everything that contributes to an ideal scientific consensus is, in the end, a moral business,[26] not more than a trust, a feeling of taking part in a community; not something that can be formalized at the end of all inquiry. Moreover:

> ... our interests shall *not* be limited. They must not stop at our own fate, but must embrace the whole community. This community, again, must not be limited, but must extend to all races of beings with whom we can come into immediate or mediate intellectual relation. (CP 2.654)

If this reading of Peirce is accepted then a pluralistic end of inquiry follows automatically unless one imposes a *1984* kind of consensus on these extra-

---

23. CP 5.443; for discussion see Gavin [1992].

24. Confer CP 6.3.

25. CP 1.49; 3.432; 6.287-317; 7.54; 7.220.

26. CP 7.87. For discussion see Delaney [1992], who emphasizes the 'social group' dimension of Peirce's views on science, arguing that for Peirce "the social and historical factors are seen to be partially constitutive of 'scientific rationality', 'scientific progress', and 'the realistic reach of science'''.

scientific matters (eliminating everybody who fails the *sociobiological* end of inquiry).

Nothing could stop a community of inquirers being content with what they all agree upon, except an appeal to how inquirers *should* behave, a "hope in the unlimited continuance of intellectual activity" (CP 2.655). That the end of inquiry is one of pluralism, is something Peirce did not explicitly deny. For example he says:[27]

> We cannot be quite sure that the community ever will settle down to an unalterable conclusion upon any given question. Even if they do so for the most part, we have no reason to think the unanimity will be quite complete, nor can we rationally presume any overwhelming *consensus* of opinion will be reached upon every question. All we are entitled to assume is in the form of a *hope*. (CP 6.610)

To push this a little bit further: The trust should be in pluralism. If not, then, as Wiggins said, the Peircean conceptual scheme articulates nothing that it is humanly possible to care about (Wiggins [1988]).

References

BIGELOW, J. [1990] 'The world essence', in: *Dialogue* 29: 205-17.

BIGELOW, J., B. Ellis and C. Lierse [1992] 'The world as one of a kind: Natural necessity and laws of nature', in: *The British Journal for the Philosophy of Science* 43: 371-88.

BOYD, R. [1989] 'What realism implies and what it does not', in: *Dialectica* 4: 5-29.

BOYD, R. [1991] 'Realism, anti-foundationalism and the enthusiasm for natural kinds', in: *Philosophical Studies* 61: 127-48.

BOYD, R., P. Gasper and J.D. Trout (eds.) [1991] *The Philosophy of Science*, Cambridge, MA: MIT Press

BRUNER, J. [1986] *Actual Minds, Possible Worlds*, Cambridge, MA: Harvard University Press.

CHURCHLAND, P.M. [1989] *A Neurocomputational Perspective*, Cambridge, MA: The MIT Press.

CLARK, S.R.L. [1991] 'How many selves make me?', in: D. Cockburn (ed.) *Human Beings*, Cambridge: Cambridge University Press, 17-34.

---

27. Confer: "True, it is conceivable that somebody else would attain to a like perfect knowledge which should conflict with ours. This is conceivable" (MS 409: 112 [1893-5]).

CURRIE, G. [1988] 'Realism in the social sciences: social kinds and social laws', in: R. Nola (ed.) *Relativism and Realism in Science*, Dordrecht: Kluwer, 205-27.

CURRIE, G. [1990] 'Supervenience, essentialism and aesthetic properties', in: *Philosophical Studies* 58: 243-57.

D'AMICO, R. [1995] 'Is disease a natural kind?', in: *The Journal of Medicine and Philosophy* 20: 551-69.

DE SOUSA, R. [1984] 'The natural shiftiness of natural kinds', in: *Canadian Journal of Philosophy* 14: 561-80.

DELANEY, C.F. [1992] 'Peirce on the social and historical dimensions of science', in: E. Mc Mullin (ed.) *The Social Dimensions of Science*, Notre Dame, IN: University of Notre Dame Press, 27-49.

DELANEY, C.F. [1995] 'Peirce on the reliability of science: A response to Rescher', in: Ketner [1995; 113-9].

DIRAC, P.A.M. [1939] 'The relation between mathematics and physics', in: *Proceedings of the Royal Society of Edinburgh* 59: 122-9.

DUPRÉ, J. [1989] 'Wilkerson on natural kinds', in: *Philosophy* 64: 248-51.

DUPRÉ, J. [1993] *The Disorder of Things: Metaphysical Foundations of the Disunity of Science*, Cambridge, MA: Harvard University Press.

ERESHEFSKY, M. [1991] 'Species, higher taxa, and the units of evolution', in: *Philosophy of Science* 58: 84-101.

EVANS-PRITCHARD, E.E. [1933-35] 'Imagery in Ngok Dinka cattle names', in: *Bulletin of the School of Oriental Studies* 7: 623-8.

FLANAGAN, O. [1995] 'Deconstructing dreams: The spandrels of sleep', in: *The Journal of Philosophy* 92: 5-27.

FRIEDMAN, L. [1995] 'Peirce's transcendental and immanent realism', in: *Transactions of the Charles S. Peirce Society* XXXI: 375-92.

FUKUI, K. [1979] 'Cattle colour symbolism and inter-tribal homicide among the Bodi', in: *Senri Ethnological Studies* 3: 147-77.

GAVIN, W.J. [1992] *William James and the Reinstatement of the Vague*, Philadelphia: Temple University Press.

GHISELIN, M.T. [1987] 'Species concepts, individuality, and objectivity', in: *Biology and Philosophy* 2: 127-43.

GOODMAN, N. [1972] *Problems and Projects*, Indianapolis, IN: Bobbs-Merrill.

GRAYBOSCH, A.J. [1992] 'Abduction, justification, and realism', in: E.C. Moore (ed.) *Charles S. Peirce and the Philosophy of Science*, Tuscaloosa, AL: The University of Alabama Press, 89-104.

GRIFFITHS, P.E. [1996] 'Darwinism, process structuralism, and natural kinds', in: *Philosophy of Science* 63: 31-9.

HAACK, S. [1992] 'Extreme scholastic realism: Its relevance to philosophy of science today', in: *Transactions of the Charles S. Peirce Society* XXVIII: 19-50.

HACKING, I. [1991] 'A tradition of natural kinds', in: *Philosophical Studies* 61: 109-26; 149-154.

HIRSCH, E. [1982] *The Concept of Identity*, New York: Oxford University Press.

HIRSCH, E. [1993] *Dividing Reality*, New York: Oxford University Press.

HOOKWAY, C. [1985] *Peirce*, London and New York: Routledge.

HORGAN, T. [1982] 'Supervenience and microphysics', in: *Pacific Philosophical Quarterly* 63: 29-43.

HULSWIT, M. [1997] 'Peirce's teleological approach to natural classes', in: *Transactions of the Charles S. Peirce Society* XXXIII: 722-72.

JOHNSON, D.M. [1990] 'Can abstractions be causes?', in: *Biology and Philosophy* 5: 63-77.

KAPITAN, T. [1992] 'Peirce and the autonomy of abductive reasoning', in: *Erkenntnis* 37: 1-26.

KETNER, K.L. [1995] *Peirce and Contemporary Thought: Philosophical Inquiries*, New York: Fordham University Press.

KITCHER, P. [1984] 'Species', in: *Philosophy of Science* 51: 308-33.

KLUGE, A.G. [1990] 'Species as historical individuals', in: *Biology and Philosophy* 5: 417-31.

KRIPKE, S. [1980] *Naming and Necessity*, Oxford: Blackwell.

LOWE, E.J. [1991] 'Real selves: Persons as a substantial kind', in: D. Cockburn (ed.) *Human Beings*, Cambridge: Cambridge University Press, 87-107.

MILL, J. S. [1843] 'A System of Logic', in: J.M. Robertson (ed.) *Collected Works of John Stuart Mill. Vol. 7*, Toronto: University of Toronto Press.

MILLIKAN, R.G. [1984] *Language, Thought, and Other Biological Categories: New Foundations for Realism*, Cambridge, MA: The MIT Press.

MILLIKAN, R.G. [1997] 'A common structure for concepts of individuals, stuffs, and real kinds: more mama, more milk and more mouse', in: *Behavioral and Brain Sciences*, in press.

NEEDHAM, R. [1972] *Belief, Language, and Experience*. Oxford: Blackwell.

ODDIE, G. [1991] 'Supervenience, goodness, and higher-order universals', in: *Australasian Journal of Philosophy* 69: 20-47.

PARGETTER, R. [1988] 'Goodness and redness', in: *Philosophical Papers* 17: 113-26.

PUTNAM, H. [1975] 'The meaning of meaning', in: *Philosophical Papers. Vol. II*, Cambridge: Cambridge University press, 215-71.

QUINE, W.V. [1969] 'Natural kinds', in: *Ontological Relativity and Other Essays*, New York: Columbia University Press, 114-38.

QUINE, W.V. [1992] 'Structure and nature', in: *The Journal of Philosophy* 89: 5-9.

RAMSEY, W., S.P. Stich and D.E. Rumelhart (eds.) [1991] *Philosophy and Connectionist Theory*, Hillsdale, NJ: Lawrence Erlbaum.

RESCHER, N. [1995] 'Peirce on validation of science', in: Ketner [1995; 102-12].

ROVANE, C. [1993] 'Self-reference: The radicalization of Locke', in: *The Journal of Philosophy* 90: 73-97.

SAUNDERS, B.A.C. and J. van Brakel [1996] 'The phantom objectivity of colour: With reference to the works of Franz Boas on the Kwakiutl', in: K. Simms (ed.) *Translation of Sensitive Texts*, Amsterdam: Rodopi, 87-95.

SAUNDERS, B.A.C. and J. van Brakel [1997] 'Are there non-trivial constraints on colour categorisation?', in: *Behavioral and Brain Sciences* 20: 167-232.

SAVELLOS, E. [1992] 'Criteria of identity and the individuation of natural-kind events', in: *Philosophy and Phenomenological Research* 52: 807-31.

SEARLE, J.R. and D. Vanderveken (1985) *Foundations of Illocutionary Logic*, Cambridge: Cambridge University Press.

SPLITTER, L.J. [1988] 'Species and identity', in: *Philosophy of Science* 55: 323-48.

STALKER, D. (ed.) [1994] *Grue*, La Salle: Open Court.

VAN BRAKEL, J. [1986] 'The chemistry of substances and the philosophy of natural kinds', in: *Synthese* 69: 291-324.

VAN BRAKEL, J. [1991] 'Meaning, prototypes and the future of cognitive science', in: *Minds and Machines* 1: 233-57.

VAN BRAKEL, J. [1992] 'Natural kinds and manifest forms of life', in: *Dialectica* 46: 243-63.

VAN BRAKEL, J. [1993] 'Peirce's pragmatisch realisme', in: M. Hulswit and H.C.D.G. de Regt (eds.) *Tekenen van Waarheid: C.S. Peirce en de Hedendaagse Wetenschapsfilosofie*, Tilburg: Tilburg University Press, 175-206.

VAN BRAKEL, J. [1997] 'Chemistry as the science of the transformation of substances', in: *Synthese* 111: 253-82.

WESTPHAL, J. [1987] *Colour: Some Philosophical Problems from Wittgenstein*, Oxford: Basil Blackwell.

WIGGINS, D. [1988] 'Truth, invention, and the meaning of life', in: G. Sayre-McCord (ed.) *Essays on Moral Realism*, Ithaca: Cornell University Press, 127-65.

WILKERSON, T. [1988] 'Natural kinds', in: *Philosophy* 63: 29-42.

WILKERSON, T. [1995] *Natural Kinds*, Aldershot: Avebury.

WILLIAMS, M.B. [1985] 'Species are individuals: theoretic foundations for the claim', in: *Philosophy of Science* 52: 578-591.

THE IMPORTANCE OF BEING EARNEST:
SCEPTICISM AND THE LIMITS OF FALLIBILISM
IN PEIRCE

LUCIANO FLORIDI

> *Jack: "Can you doubt it, Miss Fairfax?"*
> *Gwendolen: "I have the gravest doubts upon the*
> *subject. But I intend to crush them. This is not*
> *the moment for German scepticism. Their*
> *explanations appear to be quite satisfactory,*
> *especially Mr. Worthing's. That seems to me to*
> *have the stamp of truth upon it."*
>
> (Oscar Wilde, *The Importance of Being Earnest*,
> Act III)

1. OPENING[1]

The trouble with scepticism is that it is the kind of embarrassing company any thoughtful epistemology would rather bid farewell to, than welcome. That some critical philosophies appear to have profited from a clever intercourse with sceptical doubts only reinforces this initial impression: epistemologists may fancy scepticism, but they inevitably end up marrying dogmatism. Thus, the most serious charge one can level at a theory of knowledge is not that of having passionately indulged in radical doubts in its prime, but of being less than completely faithful to its anti-sceptical vow once it has reached full maturity. The intellectual tension underlying this process is obvious: a theory of knowledge is expected both to take advantage of sceptical questions in order to uproot itself from intellectual dullness, and to acquire, in so doing, all the conceptual resources necessary to avoid being led astray by nonsensical doubts. The skill consists precisely in being sufficiently critical without being utterly blinded by criticism.

In philosophers such as Descartes, Berkeley or Hegel the dialectical tension, and the conceptual resources demanded to resolve it, are in the foreground and hence we can appreciate them almost immediately. In others,

---

1. I am grateful to all the participants in the International Symposium on Peirce, organized by the Institute of Philosophy, University of Leuven (23-24 May, 1997), for their suggestions and criticisms of a previous draft of this paper. I am especially indebted to Guy Debrock and Jaap van Brakel for their comments, which have prompted me to investigate Peirce's scientific fallibilism further.

like Locke, Kant and Peirce himself, both tension and resources tend to lie in the background, not so much because they are felt to be less urgent, but rather because they come to be concealed from the reader's immediate view by logically subsequent issues and theories, which are sometimes only apparently more pressing. In Peirce's case, which interests us most here, the concealing feature is the profoundly anti-Cartesian nature of his philosophy. Some preparatory investigation is therefore required to disentangle the sceptical tension from Peirce's criticism of Descartes' methodological doubt, and make it visible, on its own, with sufficient sharpness. What does Peirce mean by scepticism, apart from Cartesian methodological scepticism? The very way in which I phrase the question anticipates the fact that there is indeed more than one sense in which Peirce speaks of sceptical theories. Having clarified as much, the next task is to elucidate whether Peirce always takes an unequivocal and consistent attitude towards all types of scepticism. Is Peirce a downright anti-sceptic? Again, it will soon be seen that the correct answer needs to be more qualified than is usually deemed necessary. Once the tension is thus brought to light, a critical assessment of the resources devised to resolve it is in order. We shall see that Peirce is, quite conclusively, a committed anti-sceptic in the most significant sense of the word - if Peirce's philosophy fails to qualify as anti-sceptical than everyone's does - but how far can Peirce's fallibilism be claimed to succeed in entirely divorcing itself from a sceptical outlook? That Peirce is adverse to almost every form of scepticism is a fact. That his fallibilism succeeds in taming the sceptical challenge without also being significantly affected by it can be argued only on account of the metaphysical price his philosophy is ready to accept. It is a price so great that it seems that no other version of fallibilism is inclined to pay it these days.

2. FIRST ACT: WHAT DOES PEIRCE MEAN BY SCEPTICISM?

Drawing up a chronological table of places in Peirce's *Collected Papers*, where sceptical topics are either mentioned or discussed in a significant manner, is probably the best way to start clarifying the several different meanings that Peirce attaches to the word 'scepticism' (Table 1). The list of passages is far from exhaustive, but it is adequate to illustrate the various typologies. Each form of scepticism now deserves a brief comment.

(A) Cartesian doubt / faked scepticism - which Peirce considers to be:
    (1)   extreme and in the spirit of Cartesianism;
    (2)   not genuine, since it provides no positive, convincing reasons for really doubting specific classes of beliefs;
    (3)   self-deceptive, speculative and impossible to achieve;
    (4)   useless and deceitful, because we seem to be challenging all our beliefs by a *fiat* while, in fact, by casting general

doubt on all we do not seriously challenge any single belief;

(5)   apparently progressive, in truth conservative, it is only a first step towards the re-acceptance of all our beliefs;

(6)   solipsistic, because it is not inter-subjective (it does not arise from discussion with other members of the epistemic community, nor from the epistemic intercourse with reality); but infra-subjective, i.e. an intellectual solitaire, self-imposed, unnatural and, by definition, incapable of solution.

	1868	1868	1873	1885	1896	1903	1903	1905
A	CP 5.264 -265	CP 5.318 -319						
B		5.318 -319 5.327		CP 8.39 8.46		CP 1.18		
C			CP 7.315	8.43 -45		1.344		CP 5.451
D				8.45 8.51 -52				
E					CP 6.493	1.344		
F					6.493	1.18 -19		
G							CP 5.96	

Table 1: Peirce's descriptions of scepticism - a taxonomy[2]

2. The dated columns, from left to right, are respectively taken from the following documents and scripts written by Peirce: 'Some Consequences of Four Incapacities', *Journal of Speculative Philosophy*, 1868 (part of *The Search for Method*, 1893); 'Grounds of Validity of the Laws of Logic: Further Consequences of Four Incapacities', *Journal of Speculative Philosophy*, 1868 (part of *The Search for Method*, 1893); 'Logic', 1873; Review of J. Royce's *The Religious Aspect of Philosophy*, 1885; a fragment on knowledge of God, 1896; from the Lowell Lectures of 1903; 'Issues of Pragmaticism', *The Monist*, 1905.

(B) Absolute scepticism:

(1)   considers every argument and never decides upon its validity;

(2)   is not refutable, since it is based on the logical possibility of counterfactuals, such as "nothing can be proved beyond the possibility of doubt" and "no argument could be legitimately used against an absolute sceptic" (CP 5.327);

(3)   although often accused of being self-contradictory, is perfectly consistent;

(4)   is impossible (there are no absolute sceptics);

(5)   is possibly different from Cartesian doubt in so far as the latter is considered a deceptive method, as Peirce says that "I am neither addressing absolute sceptics, nor men in any state of fictitious doubt whatever" (CP 5.319);

(6)   is a dialectical method (e.g. in Royce's: *The Religious Aspect of Philosophy*), when it is employed to challenge the most fundamental beliefs.

Peirce considers absolute scepticism, like Cartesian hyperbolic doubt, a fruitless and deceptive way of carrying on a philosophical investigation.

(C) Constructive / moderate scepticism:

(1)   scepticism is constructive if and only if it satisfies four conditions:

(1.1)   it is based on sincere and real doubt;

(1.2)   it is aggressive towards established beliefs, it is a "masculine" form of scepticism (CP 1.344), especially when the former have a nominalist nature (sceptics are the best friends of spiritual truth);

(1.3)   it is fruitful, i.e. by challenging established beliefs it is a source of intellectual innovation and promotes inquiry, and;

(1.4)   it is tolerant and ready to acknowledge what it doubts as soon as the doubted element comes clearly to light;

(2)   represents the life of investigation, since when all doubts are set at rest inquiry must stop;

(3)   it is therefore one of the intellectual forces behind the advancement of knowledge, which can critically unsettle the system of beliefs, for "scepticism about the reality of things, - provided it be genuine and sincere, and not a sham, - is a healthful and growing stage of mental development" (CP 8. 43) and supports the "Will to Learn" (CP 5.583).

(D) Ethical scepticism:

    (1)   is the pragmatic (i.e. ethical and religious) counterpart of Cartesian scepticism (a make-believe position), as people cannot doubt their beliefs at will, let alone their moral values and certainties.

(E) Anti-scientific and conservative scepticism:

    (1)   means doubting the validity of elementary ideas;

    (2)   amounts to a proposal to turn an idea out of court and allow no further inquiry into its value and applicability;

    (3)   is a mendacious, clandestine, disguised and conservative variety of scepticism, which is afraid of truth; since nothing goes, then anything goes, and tradition becomes the ultimate and only criterion of evaluation;

    (4)   obstructs inquiry and is to be condemned as anti-scientific by the fundamental principle of scientific method.

(F) Nominalist, anti-realist scepticism:

    (1)   only nominalists indulge in anti-scientific scepticism, as "Neither can I think that a certain action is self-sacrificing, if no such thing as self-sacrifice exists, although it may be very rare. It is the nominalists, and the nominalists alone, who indulge in such scepticism, which the scientific method utterly condemns" (CP 6.493);

    (2)   is akin to anti-scientific and conservative scepticism, since nominalists and anti-realists are ready to turn an idea out of court and allow no further inquiry into its applicability.

(G) Theoretical blindness:

    (1)   to be a sceptic means to be blinded by theory and fall into a form of intellectualism of a Cartesian or nominalist kind.

Even without recalling Peirce's famous critique of Cartesianism, in his 1868 *Journal of Speculative Philosophy* papers, this schematic survey suffices to show that, initially, Peirce's understanding of scepticism was closely coupled with his discussion of Cartesian epistemology, but that it became more and more articulated through the years, until it was fully absorbed into his technical vocabulary.

From the analysis of Cartesian doubt a position is developed which amounts to absolute scepticism and of which the other forms of scepticism listed in the last four positions (ethical, anti-scientific, nominalist, theoretical) are further variations. There can be no doubts regarding Peirce's rejection of absolute or Cartesian scepticism. One only needs to recall that, for Descartes, the hyperbolic doubt is a means to clear the ground for static foundations of a new 'dogmatism', a vital element in the internal monologue of the single mind and an essential step towards individualism and the subject's epistemic responsibility. Whereas for Peirce a genuine form of doubt is a falsificationist means to keep the road of inquiry constantly open, a vital element in the deontology of scientific communication and an essential step towards the construction of a community of scientific inquirers less fallible than any of its members.

But the dynamic process of investigation, which permeates Peirce's whole philosophy, makes him aware of the importance and utility of a constructive form of scepticism. It is thanks to a radical form of doubt that in 'The Fixation of Belief' we can move from the method of tenacity (dogmatically holding fast to one's beliefs), to the method of authority (deferring to someone else the right to assess the epistemic value of a belief), to the *a priori* method (the intra-subjective way of coming to the acceptance of a belief without taking into account either reality or other people's minds), to the scientific method (the inter-subjective way of coming to an agreement about the acceptability of a belief, further constrained by reality). Inquiry is really prompted only by further genuine doubts of external origin. Peirce defends an 'externalist' theory of doubt on the basis of a psychological analysis which first identifies, rather controversially, doubt with surprise. But then he correctly negates the possibility of giving oneself a genuine surprise and settles for a constructive scepticism, which shows the importance of being earnest in the pursuit of knowledge.[3] It is now that, in view of the role played by genuine doubts, one may wonder whether Peirce, who is certainly not an extreme sceptic, may nevertheless qualify as a moderate one.

3. SECOND ACT: IS PEIRCE'S PHILOSOPHY A MODERATE FORM OF SCEPTICISM?

Peirce rejects absolute scepticism as a methodology (Cartesian scepticism), as an anthropology (Pyrrhonian blessed state of ignorance), as an ontology (irreconcilable dualism, nominalism, anti-realism) and as an epistemology (indirect knowledge, dualism). But he appreciates it as a deontological stance, and when this is combined with his strong fallibilism it is easy to mistake him for a moderate sceptic, for some of the things that constitute his fallibilism may, at first sight, appear to be mere rewording of sceptical doctrines.

Examples abound, so I shall limit myself to just a few classic quotations:

> I will not, therefore, admit that we know anything whatever with *absolute* certainty. (CP 7.108)

---

3. See for example CP 5.443.

All positive reasoning is of the nature of judging the proportion of something in a whole collection by the proportion found in a sample. Accordingly, there are three things to which we can never hope to attain by reasoning, namely absolute certainty, absolute exactitude and absolute universality. We cannot be absolutely certain that our conclusions are even approximately true; for the sample may be utterly unlike the unsampled part of the collection. We cannot pretend to be even approximately exact; because the sample consists of but a finite number of instances and only admits special values of the proportion sought. Finally, even if we could ascertain with absolute certainty and exactness that the ratio of sinful men to all men was as 1 to 1; still among the infinite generations of men there would be room for any finite number of sinless men without violating the proportion. The case is the same with a seven legged calf. Now if exactitude, certitude, and universality are not to be attained by reasoning, there is certainly no other means by which they can be reached. (CP 1.142)

Besides positive science can only rest on experience; and experience can never result in absolute certainty, exactitude, necessity or universality. (CP 1.55)

On the whole, then, we cannot in any way reach perfect certitude or exactitude. We can never be absolutely sure of anything, nor can we with any probability ascertain the exact value of any measure or general ratio. This is my conclusion after many years of study of the logic of science. (CP 1.147)

We could easily extend the selection, but I believe it is already sufficient to make my point clear: out of its context, Peirce's fallibilism may look dangerously similar to a sceptical position. That it fails to qualify as one, however, is due to the fact that none of the following three theses, which a philosophy should endorse, at least as its implicit consequences, to count as a sceptical philosophy, would be acceptable for Peirce, namely:

(1)   knowledge is unattainable;
(2)   truth - as the ultimate description of the essential nature of the object under investigation - is unreachable;
(3)   and justification of a synthetic nature (i.e. not merely analytic) is impossible.

Peirce can reject (1), although he accepts that *infallible* and **certain** knowledge is unattainable, because he re-interprets scientific knowledge as a cognitive process of constant approximation and gradual convergence towards the ultimate truth. The precise features of such 'convergent realism' are far from being altogether clear even in Peirce himself, but for our present purpose we may say that, for Peirce, although human knowledge has a socio-historical basis and always remains perfectible, this is not equivalent to saying that scientific inquiry is not progressive nor cumulative.

Peirce can reject (2), although he is willing to qualify truth as the regulative limit towards which knowledge is constantly proceeding, because he abandons an imagist conception of it. Ultimate truth is indeed unattainable, but not unapproachable. On the contrary, scientific truth is precisely what regulates the dynamic of scientific investigations from outside, while truth in a more ordinary sense - i.e., as qualifying ordinary statements and not understood as the final point of convergence of a perfect community of investigators - acquires a gradual nature in so far as it is translated in terms of increasing degrees of adequacy of knowledge to its own reference.

Finally, Peirce can reject (3) because he accepts that justification is not a matter of single and rigid chains of inferences, but of adaptable networks of supporting reasons, which can undergo modification, and usually improve but can sometimes deteriorate, without necessarily collapsing, thus abandoning the individualist approach, fostered by Descartes, in favor of social interaction. For Peirce, science provides probable statements and law-like generalizations which are improving indefinitely, almost as if to allow us a never-ending pleasure in scientific discovery: theories are progressive, cumulative and convergent in the long run, self-correcting and, hence, never rigidly established; they evolve from being plausible to being likely, to being practically certain. As a result, Peirce's meta-interpretation of scientific knowledge is highly optimistic - our degree of ignorance is constantly decreasing through time - and could not be further removed from even a moderate form of scepticism.

4. THIRD ACT: IS PEIRCE'S FALLIBILISM SUCCESSFUL AGAINST SCEPTICISM?

4.1 Peirce's Fallibilism

Once Peirce's anti-scepticism has been singled out from its anti-Cartesian components and the several ways in which he understands a sceptical position are seen to be leading to a plain rejection - with the exception only of an explicit appreciation of a deontological kind of scepticism, i.e., of a critical and constructive way of raising sincere doubts and fruitful questions - there still remains a fundamental problem to consider. Peirce's epistemology is clearly not sceptical, but does his falsificationism have sufficient resources not just to withstand but to undermine scepticism? What are the grounds and the arguments that enable Peirce to reject scepticism? Although some of them are rather implicit, the anti-sceptical arguments put forward by Peirce's fallibilist position seem to be reducible to a combination of the following four components: the ontological, the epistemic, the *consensus omnium* and the anthropological argument.

4.2 The Ontological Argument

In brief terms: there is an external reality affecting the mind. That there is an external reality is shown, according to Peirce, by a phenomenological proof: the undeniable clash between mind and reality, which everyone is constantly experiencing and must be aware of. However, an initial dualism 'mind vs. reality' (whose absence Peirce rightly believes to be the main shortcoming of Hegel's idealism), would be welcomed by the sceptic; indeed it is a necessary condition for any form of scepticism. Both Peirce and the sceptic may agree on the presence of an overwhelming impression of independent 'otherness', felt by all subjects whenever they are dealing with external reality. This may not be under discussion. It is rather the possibility of knowing such external reality that raises epistemic problems. Peirce's ontological realism thus needs to be further reinforced by a theory of cognition and an appeal both to the *consensus omnium* argument and to the anthropological argument.

4.3 The Epistemic Argument

In brief terms: in having experience of the external reality the mind is directly affected in an informative and reliable way. Peirce's 'presentational', as opposed to 'representational', position can work as a form of direct realism, allowing him to modify the initial dualism into a bridged dualism or, better still, a *bilateral monism*.[4] The representationist holds that "percepts stand for something behind them", while the presentationist holds that:

> ... perception is a two-sided [i.e. bilateral] consciousness
> in which the percept appears as forcibly acting upon us, so
> that in perception the consciousness of an active object
> and of a subject acted on are as indivisible as, in making
> a muscular effort, the sense of exertion is one with and
> inseparable from the sense of resistance. (CP 5.607)

However, the fact that, according to a presentational theory of knowledge,

---

4. This is largely Peirce's terminology (CP 5.607).

an object can exist both as something in the world and as a percept in the mind only helps to explain Peirce's rejection of scepticism, rather than justifying it.

4.4 The Consensus Omnium Argument

In brief terms: knowledge is a social enterprise (inter-subjectivity thesis) and truth is what the community of knowers will be able to agree upon if the inquiry is pursued for long enough (evolutionary thesis). We know that the *consensus omnium* is precisely what Descartes fights (anti-traditionalism) and that, without further support, Peirce can employ it only as a negative constraint or a 'test-bed'. Whatever inquirers sincerely *disagree* about still requires further investigation, so the *lack* of *consensus* is epistemologically significant and (negatively) conclusive. However, it is also obvious that all inquirers may be able to agree on a particular selection of scientific statements for as long as we might want to imagine and yet still miss the truth, so the *presence* of an increasing *consensus* of all generations of inquirers *per se* may be significant but is very far from being (positively) conclusive (of course, this is just another way of formulating the problem facing inductive inferences). Thus, the epistemological value of the *consensus omnium* can be ultimately decisive only if the anthropological argument can be defended.

4.5 The Anthropological Argument

In brief terms: the pursuit of knowledge is a positive, innate feature of all human minds, which have a natural instinct for guessing right, corresponding to the intelligibility of the world.

For Peirce, and contrary to the sceptic's position, not only:

      (1)   is scientific inquiry the natural end of human nature,[5] but

---

5. Science "does not consist so much in *knowing*, nor even in "organized knowledge," as it does in diligent inquiry into truth for truth's sake, without any sort of axe to grind, nor for the sake of the delight of contemplating it, but from an impulse to penetrate into the reason of things" (CP 1.44). The scientist is a person who "burns to learn and sets himself to comparing his ideas with experimental results in order that he may correct those ideas" (CP 1.44). "It is not too much to say that next after the passion to learn there is no quality so indispensable to the successful prosecution of science as imagination" (CP 1.47). For "nothing but imagination that can ever supply him an inkling of the truth ... in the absence of imagination they [phenomena] will not connect themselves together in any rational way" (CP 1.46). And in CP 1.80, Peirce stresses the fundamental importance of instinctive judgment, which he describes as an inward power not sufficient to reach the truth by itself, but yet supplying an essential factor in the influences directing the mind to the truth. This he equates with Galileo's "*il lume naturale*".

> this, by itself, would not yet count as an anti-sceptical argument, so;

(2)   the constant increase in predictive success, manipulative control and explanatory power of science is tantamount to its empirical adequacy because the human natural "instinct" for guessing right is "strong enough not to be overwhelmingly more often wrong than right" (CP 5.173).[6]

Such an insight (Peirce also calls it *natural light*, or *light of nature*, or *instinctive insight*, or *genius*)[7] is a kind of epistemic instinct or faculty of divining the ways of Nature. But what justifies (2)? Peirce seems to have in mind three main reasons, for he holds that:

(1)   (2) happens to be the case due to evolutionary history (based on the history of science) and the adaptive value of such an instinct;[8] it is a *post-facto* necessity (we would not be here asking that very question if (2) were not the case), the result of the evolutionary necessity of organic survival;

(2)   (2) can be the case because nature and mind do not differ sharply, "it is a primary hypothesis underlying all abduction that the human mind is akin to the truth in the sense that in a finite number of guesses it will light upon the correct hypothesis" (CP 7.220);[9]

(3)   (2) ought to be the case if the desire to know is combined with a semeiotic theory which recognizes, as it should, that even the lack of information and the presence of mistakes can be a source of knowledge. This is why a community of inquirers is naturally led to generate knowledge in the long run. Science is self-correcting.

For all these reasons, Peirce's position appears to be very close to *scholastic monism*: as natural beings we have a fairly reliable way of entering into the world's secrets and the self-correcting nature of scientific inquiry is based on the openness of nature to the mind. If even chickens are endowed with an innate tendency towards a positive truth, there is no reason to think that this gift should be completely denied to man alone.[10]

---

6. See also CP 5.174 and CP 5.181.

7. CP 5.604.

8. CP 2.749-54; 6.418

9. For other restatements of the same point see, for example, CP 5.522 and CP 5.604.

10. CP 5.591.

4.6 Perceptual Knowledge

Peirce's epistemological 'continuism' or naturalism, in line with his anti-dualism, and his conception of a harmonic relation between mind and reality, appear more clearly when perceptual knowledge is under scrutiny. Our perceptual judgements are inevitable because they are uncontrolled. They are micro-inferences, but subconscious and automatic. A *percept* forces itself upon the mind and it is present as a *percipuum* in a perceptual judgement. A perceptual judgement is "a judgement asserting in propositional form what a character of a percept directly present to the mind is" (CP 5.54). It is reality's blow, and it is not believed or disbelieved, certain or uncertain, true or false, it is simply directly and inevitably experienced, although not passively, since it is subject to complex mental transformations. The inevitability of percepts makes them indubitable; they cannot be called into question, for "perceptual judgements are to be regarded as an extreme case of abductive inferences, from which they differ in being absolutely beyond criticism" (CP 5.181).[11]

But what is it that justifies us in believing that such perceptual judgements capture the intrinsic nature of their references? That they are unconscious and indubitable, not subject to further criticism but forced upon us by reality does not yet mean that they are always epistemologically trustworthy. What makes them an initially reliable ground for knowledge is their relational nature: on the one hand, they are utterly objective because the *percipuum* is just the percept as existing in the mind; and, on the other hand, the mind is endowed with the innate capacity for taking full epistemic advantage of such *percepta*. Of course, to say that perceptual judgements are indubitable does not mean that they are necessarily infallible or incorrigible, and this is why the inter-subjective experience of a multitude of inquirers is crucial. The more individuals that test and confirm a particular experience the more unlikely error becomes, and this is not due to a fallacious reliance on some elementary inductive reasoning, but because individuals, though fallible, have an absolutely crucial tendency to get things right.

5. CONCLUSION: WHAT PEIRCE'S ANTI-SCEPTICISM CAN TEACH US

Peirce's anti-scepticism appears to be based, in the end, on a strong metaphysical position, namely the postulation of a reliable communication between being and mind, and the rejection, as utterly unreasonable, of an irrecoverable, static dichotomy between man and a mechanized, soul-less universe, as if there were a wall of silence between the two which made reality unknowable and unintelligible. Of course, many 'philosophical

---

11. See also CP 5.116.

characters' could not disagree more deeply with such a view: the sceptic himself, the Kantian philosopher, the existentialist, and the relativist, to name just a few.

I believe they are right, but it is not with this particular problem that I wish to close this paper. In an important and common sense of the word 'understanding' at least, Peirce seems to be right in acknowledging that "unless man has a natural bent in accordance with nature's, he has no chance of understanding nature at all" (CP 6.477). He appears to believe that the history of science provides plenty of evidence to vindicate the presence of such a "natural bent". Peirce's metaphysical view of man's organic position in the world is what allows his fallibilism to be a version of realism (knowledge is increasingly achievable and it is knowledge of the world in itself), rather than instrumentalism (knowledge works, and the world is at least compatible with scientific theories), and I take this to be a most interesting suggestion contained in his anti-scepticism.

A fallibilism which does not attribute the source of its success to nature itself, e.g. by endorsing some theory of a "natural bent", cannot be thoroughly faithful to its profession of anti-scepticism. The presence of reality can assure empirical restraint and hence practical reliability, but not insightful comprehension of the object of knowledge and then true understanding. When lacking a metaphysical ground, versions of falsificationism such as Neurath's, Popper's or Quine's are forced to abandon the initial assumption that reliable and inter-subjectively acceptable beliefs are actually capturing the intrinsic nature of their ontic counterpart. What has Neurath's raft got to do with the sea, Popper's pile house with the swamp, or Quine's fabric/force field with the environment? Science becomes a systemic, holistic set of statements which, lacking a firm and direct channel of communication with its external reference, also lacks a direct correspondence with nature. Without a strong metaphysics such as Peirce's the view of a progressive, cumulative converging, a more and more adequately true science is no longer ontologically justified. Reality at most indirectly constrains but does not inform, and knowledge becomes a matter of signs, not of indices (which cannot change), nor of icons (which are isomorphic). Changed weather means a different flag, but the flag is a mere convention indicating the weather; it does not capture its nature. Fallibilist systems can be well structured, but lacking the assurance that mind and being are truly communicating they stand before the world as a separate, constantly revisable manifold of laws and empirical statements. Their indexical components (Neurath's protocols, Popper's observations, Quine's observation sentences) are the most basic, but because they too are revisable, though with more difficulty, then, since we assume that their references remain stable, we must infer they are not really in touch with it.

The flag can be replaced by a whistle. Science is only indeterminately linked with reality, but does not describe it as it is in itself. Without an anti-dualist principle, such as Peirce's 'natural bent' and his theory of direct cognition, the connection between science and reality may well be just one of constrained construction of a system of laws and experiential statements which may still be far from capturing the essential nature of their references.

Back to Peirce then? Not quite, for unfortunately a last problem remains. It is not by chance that fallibilism has recently developed towards a non-metaphysical and instrumentalist position. As Gwendolen would put it, the twentieth century may not be the moment for absolute scepticism, but it is no longer time for medieval optimism either, because Peirce's and other similar views are far too intellectualist. We only need to recall his phenomenological method to be able to show, quite easily, that man is not so earnest about inquiry, let alone naturally bent on knowing the world. Fallibilism cannot retreat to a metaphysical trench of a Peircean kind to escape its instrumentalist fate, it can only move forward towards a full acceptance of its constructionist nature. This is the direction in which, more or less consciously, contemporary philosophy is moving.

REASON AND INSTINCT

MICHAEL VAN HEERDEN

1. INTRODUCTION

On many occasions and throughout the development of his thought, Peirce envisaged one essential project for philosophy.[1] In one of his earliest papers entitled: 'Grounds of Validity of the Laws of Logic: Further Consequences of Four Incapacities', he describes this project as such:

> There can be no doubt of the importance of this problem. According to Kant, the central question of philosophy is "How are synthetical judgments *a priori* possible?" But antecedently to this comes the question how synthetical judgments in general, and still more generally, how synthetical reasoning is possible at all. When the answer to the general problem has been obtained, the particular one will be comparatively simple. This is the lock upon the door of philosophy. (CP 5.348)

The purpose of Immanuel Kant's most important book, the *Critique of Pure Reason*, was to show that, although all our knowledge is based in experience, it is, nonetheless, partly *a priori*.[2] In other words, it is not only inductively inferred from experience, but our own mental apparatus orders sensation and supplies the *a priori* concepts with which we can synthesize and understand experience. For Peirce, however:

> Kant gives the erroneous view that ideas are presented separated and then thought together by the mind. This is

---

1. CP 2.690; 4.92; 5.348; see also CP 2.31; 2.157; 3.634; 6.95.

2. Kant separates two distinctions which are confounded by Gottfried Leibniz (Kant [1992; 22 (B xvii)]): first, there is a distinction between analytic and synthetic judgments; second, there is a distinction between *a priori* and *a posteriori* (empirical) judgments. An analytic judgment is one in which the predicate in contained within the definition of the subject (e.g., a bachelor is an unmarried man); whereas a synthetic judgment is a proposition which we can only know through experience and in which the predicate adds to the knowledge of the subject (e.g., Paris is a large city). An *a priori* judgment is one which, though it may be elicited by experience, has a basis apart from experience; whereas an *a posteriori* judgment is one which is always based in experience ((Kant [1992; 41-62 (A 1-16; B 1-30)]).

his doctrine that a mental synthesis precedes every analysis. What really happens is that something is presented which in itself has no parts, but which nevertheless is analyzed by the mind, that is to say, its having parts consists in this, that the mind afterward recognizes those parts in it. (CP 1.384)

For Peirce, then, the initial task of any philosophy is twofold: first, to show how non-reflective, immediate experience is possible; second, to demonstrate how the mind is able to break up and differentiate components which are invariably given as parts of the whole meaningful structure of experience.[3] As Peirce's thought matured, he became progressively convinced that the answer to both riddles lay in the analysis of instinct.[4] By 1902, Peirce was able to declare that the transcendental method of Kant, or the analysis of "the *a priori* conditions of the possibility of practical everyday experience", should really entail an analysis of "instinctive beliefs" (CP 2.31). In this paper, I would like to explore the reasons why Peirce conceived of instinct as establishing both the possibility of immediate, conscious experience (practical everyday experience) and the ability to reason critically.

2. THE UTILITY OF INSTINCT

In recent discussions on instinct a lot of attention is focussed on two questions: first, whether the concept of instinct has any utility today; second, if we do admit 'species-specific' behavior (instinct), what is the relation between it and other forms of behavior such as learning and insight (Goldsmith [1994; 73, 104]). Frank A. Beach, in a seminal paper on instinct, has summarized very effectively the objections that many contemporary authors have to the concept of instinct (Beach [1955]). Beach begins by noting that the instinct/reason divide, as an explanation for the distinction between animal and human, goes back to antiquity and has both

---

3. A similar contention is reflected in our own time by Martin Heidegger. He notes that in order to lay the foundation of any metaphysic, one has first to reveal the internal possibility of ontology itself (Heidegger [1968; 18-22]). Both Kant and Heidegger take the concept of "transcendence" in human knowledge to mean the fundamental structure of transcendence: this structure is shown in the construction or opening of a horizon of objectivity. It is the knowledge of this transcendental behavior which provides the opening through which we can meet the objectivity of objects.

4. CP 7.378-87. While Peirce began writing about the importance of instinct as early as 1883 (CP 2.753-54, from 'A Theory of Probable Inference', dated 1883), his theory of instinct was a rather late development in his thought and the period of his greatest activity on instinct was from 1898 to 1908.

philosophical (Heraclitus and Seneca) and theological roots (Albertus Magnus and Thomas Aquinas). These reached a summit in the writings of René Descartes and his followers who introduced the divide into Modernity and "aggressively restated the existence of a man-brute dichotomy" (Beach [1955; 402]). Darwin and his followers tried to bridge this by amassing two types of evidence: first, evidence that showed the existence of human instincts; and, second, evidence that showed that non-human species were capable of rational behavior. However, as Beach notes, while the "idea of discontinuity in mental evolution was vigorously attacked", nobody thought that the problem may lie in the instinct/reason dichotomy itself (Beach [1955; 403]).

Beach believes that this dichotomy should disappear and that this is only possible if the concept of instinct is replaced by scientifically valid and useful explanations. The reasons he gives for this conclusion can be divided into two categories. The first category of arguments deals with the difficulty of classifying instinctive behavior because of the related difficulty of providing criteria that differentiate instinctive from acquired behavior. In fact, the only criteria which seems universally acceptable for instinct is that it is 'unlearned'. This brings us to the second category of arguments. Since what is unlearned can only be discovered through behavior that is learned and genes influence learning as much as other instinctive patterns, to prove behavior is unlearned is not really possible. This same problem is summed up by William S. Verplanck when he says that the "dilemma of innate or acquired seems to be one of those categorical pseudo problems that the philosopher Ryle has concerned himself with" (Verplanck [1955; 140]).

For Peirce, however, not only is there a fundamental continuity between all levels of mental evolution, so that all "are but phases of the one and the same process of the growth of reasonableness" (CP 5.4); but, the utility of the concepts of instinct and reason is more as heuristic categories that help us describe and understand the two ends of a continuum of self-controlled action.[5] In other words, Peirce meets both of Beach's objections by noting

---

5. MS 1343: 24 [1902]; CP 5.533. Peirce was lead to a form of Panpsychism in his thinking about the relation between mind and matter. "The one intelligible theory of the universe is that of objective idealism, that matter is effete mind, inveterate habits becoming physical laws" (CP 6.25). Peirce, like the majority of Panpsychists, does not claim any special faculty of perception that those who oppose the doctrine do not have. Nor does he claim that the position can be proven. Rather, the available scientific evidence does enable the theory of Panpsychism to be a serious contender. Paul Edwards says that the more systematic Panpsychists usually proceed by a twofold analogical deduction. First, although different in many respects, the very fact that in the essential vital processes of life, plant and animals forms are similar, means that "one cannot consistently attribute a psychic or soul life to animals and refuse it to plants" (*Encyclopedia of Philosophy*, 1967 ed. S.v. 'Panpsychism', by Paul Edwards). Second, because the borderline between animate and inanimate objects is not sharp, there is also good reasons to attribute an analogical likeness between the two i.e., the existence of some kind

that it is not an unlearned/learned criteria that distinguishes any action's place along this continuum, but the amount of self-control that it exhibits.[6] The unlearned/learned dichotomy is untenable: first, because all instincts are 'habits' of response that arise through learning at some stage (albeit in the past development of a species); and, second, because any new growth in behavior (learning) has to be based in the previous syntheses or instincts of a species.[7]

William Mc Dougall's analysis of what the most impartial description of instinct should entail, is a very clear introduction to the insights of Peirce. For Mc Dougall, a complete delineation of instinct would:

> ... show that instinctive action is everywhere and always, if the circumstances demand it, variable and adaptive; that instinctive action is always in some degree intelligent, or expressive of that capacity for purposive adaptation which is the essential function of mind. Even when we go so low in the scale as the simpler animalcules and protozoa, the same fact is revealed by that variation of response which is commonly called 'the procedure of trial and error'. (Mc Dougall [1922; 310])

Peirce is convinced that instinct is evidenced through all forms of life and that it is only with the advent of living forms that we have the birth of instinct. Here Peirce concurs with the idea that with the advent of instinct there is the first mode of specialization and differentiation within any living form and that this begins with the development of the reflex arc. Put slightly

---

of psychic existence in inanimate objects. This is the precise kind of deduction that Peirce follows.

6. Although Peirce gives no systematic definition of self-control, one can gleam his meaning from various texts. It would seem that the degree of self-control of any organism is determined by its developmental capacity and the openness of its behavioral scaling. Developmental capacity is the capacity that an organism has to adapt its behavior to novel situations (CP 1.348; 1.648; 5.477; 5.511; 6.498). Behavioral scaling is a term I have borrowed from E.O. Wilson (Goldsmith [1994; 110]) and denotes the ability of an organism to scale its behavior appropriately to different aspects of the environment (both internal and external). Peirce notes that "it is requisite to consider the character of things as relative to the perceptions and active powers of things ... The interest which the uniformities of Nature have for an animal measures his place in the scale of intelligence" (CP 6.406; see also CP 6.229). Ernst Mayr makes a similar observation when he notes the distinction between "open" and "closed" (CP 2.160; 5.499; 7.380) behavioral systems in instincts. A closed system is instinctive behavior which contains a "set of ready-made, predictable responses", whereas an open system is shown in "a great capacity to benefit from experience, to learn how to react to the environment, to continue adding "information" to their behavioral program" (Mayr [1997; 23]).

7. CP 3.157-9; 5.477; 5.492; 6.300.

differently, the advent of a reflex action is the first sign of self-control and the foundation for all other instincts.[8] In defining animal instinct Peirce writes:

> Animal instinct is a natural disposition, or inborn determination of the individual's Nature (his "nature" being that within him which causes his behaviour to be such as it is), manifested by a certain unity of quasi-purpose in his behaviour. (MS 1343: 21 [1902])

His use of the term 'quasi', he explains, is to differentiate instinctual behavior in other forms of life from that in human beings. But all forms of individual purpose, as opposed to the general purpose of habits in inanimate objects, can only be manifest with the facility of a reflex action, the embryo of self-control.[9] This latter point, I believe, is evidenced by Peirce's definition, on this occasion, of all forms of individual purpose:

> The final result will now be indefinitely approached no matter how the initial circumstances may be vased, or what perturbations may come in, the only possible effect of such variations being that it may take longer or less time to work out the resulting indefinite approach to a predetermined configuration. (MS 1343: 28 [1902])

If we continue this line of argument a little further, it is clear for Peirce that purpose is an operative desire within an individual. At first, this desire is extremely broad and consists in the removal of sources of irritation.[10] But, to secure this goal, the organism has to take account of an ever changing environment. Peirce even speaks here of 'sympathetical' and 'antipathetical' encounters between different habits and organisms. So, in the pursuit of the

---

8. CP 6.281; see also CP 1.266-7; 1.390; 3.157; 5.533.

9. MS 1343: 29 [1902]. Peirce was convinced that habits, that constitute reality or the universe of existing things, are undergoing a general tendency to greater habit-taking. Habit serves to "establish new features, and also bring them into harmony" with other existing realities (CP 6.300). This establishment of new features enables one to speak about habits and super-habits, or a series of systems in nature which are ordered hierarchically. At each new level, because the scope of relation is enhanced, a new essence and rationality emerges. This new habit, then, will "also function as a law governing the behavior of specific "sub-systems," and will partially determine the activities of more comprehensive, encompassing "super-systems." That is to say, the essential habit or nature of an individual may function as a "law of nature" for an individual at a lower dimensionality, while, at the same time, constituting a non-essential disposition or a partial determination of a nature of a more general system" (Raposa [1984; 162]).

10. MS 1343: 18 [1902]; CP 1.392.

predetermined configuration, this desire is forced to become more and more specific. And, in so doing, it gives birth to a hierarchy of instincts and the emerging levels of self-control.[11]

3. PEIRCE'S CLASSIFICATION OF INSTINCTS

I have noted that Beach was unable to provide any classification of instinctive behavior. Peirce, however, because he saw self-control as the key factor to understanding instinct, was able to provide a conditional classification. It would seem from his discussion on protoplasm, in his article: 'Man's Glassy Essence',[12] that the first two specific manifestations of instinct are growth (of which reproduction is a later development) and the assimilation of food.[13] These, in turn, are the foundation of all the more specific manifestations of instinct that we witness in different living forms. Throughout his writings on instinct, Peirce emphasizes the fundamental interrelationship between what Maryann Ayim calls the 'selfish' (based in the desire to assimilate food) and the 'social' (based in the desire to grow) instincts (Ayim [1974; 36]).[14] Both are, however, based in the one, fundamental, operative desire of any living organism to remove sources of irritation and preserve its essential unity. For Peirce, the former have endowed animals and people with some notions "of force, matter, space, and time"; while the latter have endowed them with some notion "of what sort of objects their fellow-beings are, and of how they will act on given occasions" (CP 2.753). So, from the first specification of individual purpose in growth and nutrition, a whole hierarchy of instincts grow up ever increasing the organism's attunement to the environment. It is this hierarchy that enables the progressive emergence of self-control and lays the foundation for different types of experience.

In a talk entitled: 'The Postulates of Geometry', presented in June, 1902, Peirce gave his longest description of this hierarchy (Figure 1). Peirce never deals specifically with the question of how the various leading and minor instincts interact to produce the systems of performance. I can only guess that, as we shall soon see, through associations of resemblance and contiguity, different patterns of inclusion, intersection and exclusion are established between them which create different patterns of self-control and experience.[15] Wallace Craig prefers to speak of instinctive activities as cycles in which one "may observe all gradations between a true reflex and a mere

---

11. CP 1.205; 5.552; 6.462.
12. CP 6.246-58.
13. CP 1.174.
14. CP 1.118; 5.586; 5.591; 6.500; 6.531; 7.39; 7.40; 7.378; 7.382.
15. CP 7.52; 7.375.

readiness to act, mere facilitation". While the "mutual exclusion of certain forms of instinctive behavior is inevitable, due to the incompatibility ... of their motor components"; nonetheless, exclusion is only one form of a variety of interactions (Craig [1918; 93]). In fact, for Craig, "in actual life the cycles and phases of cycles are multiplied and overlapped in very complex ways ... Smaller cycles are superimposed upon larger ones" (Craig [1918; 103]). In human beings, these cycles "appear in consciousness as cycles of attention, of feeling, and on valuation" (Craig [1918; 106]). Peirce is brought to exactly the same conclusion as Craig and his Primisense, Altersense and Medisense correspond generally to Craig's cycles of feeling, attention and valuation. For Peirce there is "no mode of consciousness that is not affected by instinct" (MS 1343: 23 [1902]); and all "systems of rational performance have had instinct for their first germ" (CP 7.381).

Leading Instincts

Social Instincts (Reproductive)		Selfish Instincts (Feeding / War)
	Minor Instincts	
Architectural		Cleanliness
Communication (cries, songs, facial)		Collecting
		Hibernation
Clothing (adornment, decoration)		Mechanical
		Medicine
Games		Concealment
Locomotion / Migration		Self-preservation

Figure 1: Peirce's classification of instincts or systems of performance (CP 7.378-87)

4. CONSCIOUS EXPERIENCE: PRIMISENSE, ALTERSENSE AND MEDISENSE

4.1 Division of Consciousness

As humans our only access to reality and to the workings of the human mind is through consciousness. Peirce is aware of the fact that for many centuries psychologists and thinkers have divided mind into the three categories of feeling, knowledge and will.[16] While Kant is often thought of as the instigator of the division, he had taken it from Tetens, a Leibnitzian writer who had developed the notion from the ideas of sixteenth century rhetoricians.[17] Kant, however, had limited the notion of feeling to feelings

---

16. CP 1.332; 1.350; 1.375.

17. CP 7.540. Johann Nicolaus Tetens, 1736/8 -1807; German philosopher and psychologist. For an account of Tetens' psychology see his *Philosophical Essays on Human Nature and Its Development* (2 Vols., 1777) *(Encyclopedia of Philosophy*, 1967 ed. S.v. 'Tetens').

of pleasure and pain; but Peirce takes Tetens lead in seeing it more generally as "whatever is directly and immediately in consciousness at any instant, just as it is, without regard to what it signifies, to what its parts are" (CP 7.540). He also proposes that sensation, instead of being put under the division of knowledge, should be put under the division of will, this because of "the sense of its assertiveness, of my being compelled to have it" (CP 7.543). With these changes in place, Peirce is left with what he considers a scientific classification of consciousness. As early as 1867 Peirce had proposed a threefold division in his logical categories which he called: Quality, Relation and Representation.[18] Peirce now renamed his division: Quality, Reaction and Mediation; and, for scientific precision: Firstness, Secondness and Thirdness. This last division introduced, thus, "new words without any false associations" (CP 4.3). The general contents of consciousness, then, are:

> ... first, feeling ... passive consciousness of quality, without recognition or analysis; second, consciousness of an interruption into the field of consciousness, sense of resistance, of an external fact, of another something; third, synthetic consciousness, binding time together, sense of learning, thought. (CP 1.377)

These three general contents are, for Peirce, the only clue that we have to the very "congenital tendencies of the mind" (CP 1.374); and, in this sense, they are also the constitutive elements of consciousness.[19]

4.2 Primisense

From Peirce's descriptions of the physiological basis of Firstness or Primisense it is not difficult to see that he means by it the state of feeling of any individual organism approximating a state of rest.[20] Peirce also calls this state of feeling in humans one's 'Immmediate' or 'Instantaneous' consciousness.[21]

> Feeling is neither over against me nor in me. If I have a momentary consciousness of self, that is part of the feeling. So that I am, or at any rate my immediate self-consciousness is, a part of my total feeling. (CP 7.543)

---

18. CP 1.555.
19. CP 7.551.
20. CP 1.354; 1.386; 2.711; 3.156; 6.264; 7.276; 7.551.
21. CP 1.307; 1.357; 5.289; 6.126; 6.345; 6.373; 7.672.

Since a state of rest is never completely attainable, this immediate consciousness can only be inferred. In a letter dated to Lady Welby on October, 12, 1904, Peirce describes how this inference can be made:

> The scarlet of your royal liveries, the quality itself, independently of its being perceived or remembered, is an example, by which I do not mean that you are to imagine that you do not perceive or remember it, but that you are to drop out of account that which may be attached to it in perceiving or in remembering, but which does not belong to the quality. (PW 24 [1904]; CP 8.329)

But this immediate consciousness is veiled from the introspective gaze of psychology "for the very reason that it is our immediate consciousness" (CP 1.310). As soon as we engage in introspection we set the contents of consciousness over against our attention and, thus, we are engaged in a duality which is of the nature of Altersense.

4.3 Altersense

The second division of consciousness, the sense of action and reaction, is Altersense or the appearance of Secondness. I have already noted how Peirce puts sensation into this division and so it is this aspect of consciousness that gives the sense of hereness and nowness. Peirce calls it 'Double', 'Dual' or 'Reflex' consciousness.[22] Willing (active or inhibitive), in which we encounter resistance, is the more active pole of Secondness, while sensation is its more passive pole.[23] In 1903, Peirce described this category to William James as follows:

> It comes out most fully in the shock of reaction between ego an non-ego. It is there the double consciousness of effort and resistance. That is something which cannot properly be conceived. For to conceive it is to generalize it; and to generalize it is to miss altogether the hereness and nowness which is its essence. (CP 8.266)

While it is of the nature of Firstness and Secondness to stand independently of thought, it is only as embedded in thought that Primisense and Altersense can be *thought* of. If Primisense corresponds to the state of feeling of any organism, then Altersense corresponds to the 'sympathetical' and

---

22. CP 5.52; 7.547.
23. CP 5.69.

'antipathetical' encounters with other organisms. This sense of ego and non-ego is at the root of self-consciousness, but self-consciousness only blossoms fully through mediation and, thus, implies the inferential nature of Thirdness or Medisense. Nathan Houser says that while full self-consiousness for Peirce "is fundamentally inferential and, therefore, is of the nature of thirdness"; however, its source is in Secondness in the experience "of opposition or intrusion from the "outside"... a quasi-self-consciousness that is not cognized but is fundamentally an experience" (Houser [1983; 341]).

4.4 Medisense

Medisense, or the appearance of Thirdness in our consciousness, is called variably by Peirce as 'Synthetic' or 'Reflective' consciousness.[24] It is that representational element in our experience or, put slightly differently, the apprehension of representational relations. One of Peirce's lists of the three elements of medisense (by which the self-controlled formation of habits occur) are: association, suggestion and attention.[25] I will return to these elements a bit later on. Earlier I noted that the first specification of purpose was growth and the assimilation of food; which are the basic instincts of all life. Peirce, at first, saw these elements as the physiological foundations of Medisense,[26] but later corrected himself by saying that it was even the more basic instinct to remove an irritation that founded the possibility of Medisense:

> Thus, the three fundamental kinds of consciousness, simple consciousness, dual consciousness, and synthetic consciousness, are to be explained by the three chief functions of the nervous system, its simple irritability, the movement of nervous energy, and the synthetic action of the nerves, especially habit. (MS 909: 55 [1890])

5. INSTINCT AND CRITICAL REASON

5.1 Peirce's Metaphor of the Lake

This brings us to the question of the relation between instinct and critical reason. Peirce was well aware of the duality that Descartes had introduced into Modernity.[27] His solution was to work to break down the absolute

---

24. CP 1.377; 1.383; 3.404.
25. CP 7.544-48; 7.551.
26. MS 901: 36-9 [1885].
27. CP 5.56; 5.63; 5.128; 7.407; 7.580; 8.30.

distinction between the instinctive and rational levels of the human mind, or between what he called the "intuitive" and "symbolic" aspects of knowledge.[28] When discussing human knowledge and reasoning, Peirce utilizes three models throughout his writings: the categories of being (Firstness, Secondness, Thirdness); the categories of scientific method (Induction, Deduction, Hypothesis); and the categories of semeiotics (Object, Interpretant, Sign). Most of his writings on the relation between instinct and reason utilize one of the first two models. I have chosen here to concentrate on the first model. This model I propose to place within the context of Peirce's metaphor of the lake for three reasons: first, because one is able to bring, in this metaphor, his ideas contained in the first model of reasoning together with his ideas on self-control, which are so vital to Peirce's conception of instinct; second, because one is able to situate the elements of Primisense, Altersense and Medisense within the model; and, third, because this metaphor helps to situate Peirce's ideas on the mind within contemporary models of the mind.[29]

Peirce also uses other metaphors (but less frequently) such as that of the conveyancer, the railway junction and terminus and the horse and rider.[30] In the metaphor of the lake, however, Peirce describes the mind as:

> ... a bottomless lake, whose waters seem transparent, yet into which we can clearly see but a little way. But in this water there are countless objects at different depths; and certain influences will give certain kinds of those objects an upward impulse which may be intense enough and continue long enough to bring them into the upper visible layer. After the impulse ceases they commence to sink downwards. (CP 7.547)

Within this lake, the "objects at different depths" also have different degrees of "buoyancy", "by virtue of which they are particularly apt to be brought up and held up near the surface by the inflowing percepts" (CP 7.554). These patterns of buoyancy belong "to those ideas that we call purposes" (CP 7.554). Altersense arises, we have seen, with the inception of sensation or willing. Sensation and willing is the initiation of a new "state of feeling" (CP 1.332); and, then, every "state of mind, acting under an overruling association, produces another state of mind" (CP 6.70). These overruling associations determine which sensations and desires will rise to synthetic consciousness, and which will be dealt with at lower levels of the mind.

---

28. CP 7.407.
29. CP 7.547; 7.553; 7.554.
30. CP 2.183; 6.301; 7.447.

There is, at this juncture, one crucial idea that has to be stressed. The overruling associations or patterns of buoyancy are called, by Peirce, "those ideas that we call purposes" (CP 7.554). Earlier I indicated that Peirce saw instincts as individual purposes. We shall see that the mind is comprised of many different types of associations. But, at the base of these are the associations created by the instinctive patterns. As the scope of self-control increases so does synthetic consciousness, and the more synthetic consciousness increases the more the obscure part of the mind becomes the larger part.[31] Peirce notes this by saying that "the obscure part of the mind is the principle part", that it "acts with far more unerring accuracy than the rest" and "it is almost infinitely more sensitive in its sensibilities" (CP 6.569). In the different patterns of buoyancy there is a type of overruling principle of subsidiarity which determines the trajectories of any sensation or of any willing (operative desires).[32] Peirce distinguishes between active and inhibitive willing: inhibitive in the sense of restricting the upward trajectory of some sensations or ideas.[33] Peirce explains it as follows:

> Respiration, circulation, and digestion are, depend upon it, better carried on as they are, without any meddling by Reason; and the countless little inferences we are continually making, - be they ever so defective, - are, at any rate, less ill performed unconsciously than they would be under the regimen of a captious and hypochondriac logic. (CP 7.448)

5.2 Medisense and Reason

We have already seen that the three constitutive elements of Medisense were association, suggestion and attention. Habits have grades of strength "varying from complete dissociation to inseparable association" (CP 5.477). This rule applies equally to the habits that comprise the patterns of

---

31. CP 5.263; 5.433; 5.533.

32. The principle dictates that nothing should be taken to a higher level of authority/competence, which can be resolved at a lower level. This would mean that the highest level of conscious reasoning only emerges in order to facilitate actions not achievable by the lower levels. Peirce wrote in *The Nation* in 1906: "Every race of animals is provided with instincts well adapted to its needs, and especially to strengthening the stock. It is wonderful how unerring these instincts are. Man is no exception in this respect; but man is so continually getting himself into novel situations that he needs, and is supplied with, a subsidiary faculty of reasoning for bringing instinct to bear upon situations to which it does not directly apply. This faculty is a very imperfect one in respect to fallibility; but then it is only needed to bridge short gaps" (CP 6.497; see also CP 2.178; 5.396).

33. CP 5.69. Peirce also calls this active and passive volition (inertia) (CP 1.332).

buoyancy in the mind. Peirce is very clear that there are two types of association, viz., resemblance and contiguity. Resemblances are associations built up because of the similarities in the qualities of states of feeling in the organism;[34] and it is this "association that constitutes the resemblance" (CP 4.157). Contiguity are those associations that are based on the "habits about acts of reaction" (sensation and willing - CP 4.157). At first, it seems as if Peirce believed that only associations of contiguity could be inherited or instinctual.[35] But, later he altercates that it is only associations by resemblance that are.[36] In an undated document, however, his position is more subtle and consistent:

> A great many associations of ideas are inherited. Others
> grow up spontaneously ... Many associations are merely
> accidental ... Other associations cannot be called accidental
> because it was in the nature of things that they should
> appear in sets. Thus, light and warm get associated in our
> minds because they are associated in Nature. (CP 7.550)

From this last document it is clear that both types of associations are either instinctual, or produced by the free play of thoughts in the mind, or acquired in the course of experience and reasoning. All of these habits of association and dissociation go to make up the patterns of buoyancy and also the scope of synthetic consciousness. By 1905 Peirce depicts the levels of association and emergent self-control as:

> ... inhibitions and coördinations that entirely escape
> consciousness. There are, in the next place, modes of
> self-control which seem quite instinctive. Next, there is a
> kind of self-control which results from training. Next, a
> man can be his own training-master and thus control his
> self-control. (CP 5.533)

This control that we exercise over our thoughts in synthetic consciousness or reasoning, "consists in our purpose holding certain thoughts up where they can be scrutinized" (CP 7.554). These thoughts that enter are either perceptual facts (the body's product of sensations that have risen to synthetic consciousness) or ideas which have risen spontaneously from the free-play

---

34. Peirce, for example, mentions the association in feeling that could be made between red and the blare of a trumpet (CP 1.314).

35. CP 7.445-6.

36. CP 4.157; 7.498-9.

of thoughts in the mind.[37] Then, by suggestion or attention, we can control the processes of thought. Peirce did not like the term suggestion, because it had connotations of hypnotism.[38] Nonetheless, when a thought rises to consciousness it "gives an upward motion to all other ideas belonging to the same set" and these are more easily available for scrutiny (CP 7.549). Attention (abstraction or contemplation),[39] is described by Peirce as:

> ... using our self-control to remove us from the forcible intrusion of other thoughts, and in considering the interesting bearings of what may lie hidden ... to cause the subjective intensity of it to increase. (CP 7.555)

Attention is a separative process by which the more general elements of each perceptual fact are drawn out.[40] These are compared with the contents of memory and a judgment follows which either leads to new associations in the mind (which alter or change old associations) or the reinforcement of old associations.[41] Peirce is clear that attention "produces affects on the nervous system" and that these affects are new habits or "nervous associations" (CP 5.297). It is, then, this cumulative process by which our culture and belief patterns are built up, that Peirce conceives as the progress of thought.

5.3 Medisense and Culture

As I noted at the outset, for Peirce the action of the human intellect, unlike in Kant, is not primarily synthetic, but analytic: that is, to break up and differentiate components which, on the level of non-reflective, immediate experience, are invariably given as parts of a whole, meaningful structure.[42] It is our ability to differentiate and combine these components in new and creative ways that enables humans to effectively create and manipulate symbols. Peirce never deals at any length with the development

---

37. CP 2.141; 7.555.

38. CP 7.548.

39. CP 7.544.

40. CP 1.353; 5.248; 7.544. It should not be thought here that any perceptual fact or qualia is only one association of the mind, but, rather, it is a cluster of such associations. "Our minds, being considerably adapted to the inner world, the ideas of feelings attract one another in our minds, and, in the course of our experience of the inner world, develop general concepts. What we call sensible qualities are such clusters" (CP 4.157).

41. CP 3.160; see also CP 1.146; 2.142; 2.252; 2.435; 2.444; 2.548; 2.773; 4.53; 4.55; 4.235; 4.541; 5.29; 5.54; 5.115; 5.157; 5.181; 5.255; 5.307; 5.569; 6.472; 7.198; 7.360.

42. CP 1.384; 4.85; 4.232; 6.225; 6.378; 6.595; 7.426.

of the human instincts.[43] Nonetheless, he makes two interesting suggestions. The first is that the unique development of humans is accounted for by an open instinct program which he calls "plastic", one that has been forced to build up countless new associations because of changing environments.[44] The instinct to feed (selfish instinct) has lead to conjectures that establish a "virtual knowledge of space and force" in many organisms (CP 5.586).

> But, as that animal would have an immense advantage in the struggle for life whose mechanical conceptions did not break down in a novel situation (such as development must bring about), there would be a constant selection in favor of more and more correct ideas of these matters. Thus would be attained the knowledge of that fundamental law upon which all science rolls; namely, that forces depend upon relations of time, space, and mass. (CP 6.418)

The second suggestion is that Peirce is convinced that the "Social Instincts were more sympathetic to Reason" (CP 7.384); these require "all the higher animals to have some insight into what is passing in the minds of their fellows" (CP 7.40).[45] Peirce believed in both embryonic and post-natal recapitulation; the latter being that a child, in its mental development, passes through the stages that our hominid ancestors passed through in their "adult development" (CP 3.488; 5.522). Be that as it may, both the demands of the social instincts and selfish instincts have forced humans to progress and refine their instincts through many new associations.[46] This refinement led to a stage of social domestication in which language was born.[47] Peirce saw that language began as a form of mimicry of natural sounds; but with the

---

43. CP 1.225; 5.480; 6.475; 7.446.

44. CP 7.381; see also CP 1.638; 2.178; 5.511; 6.498. Many contemporary authors see the importance of the challenge of surviving in the open savannah climate of Africa, after the shrinking of the tropical forests, as a vital stage in hominid development (Johanson [1991; 262]; Leakey [1993; 164]). Others have also mentioned the essentially open nature of hominid instinctive programs and morphology as essential to the development of hominids (Marais [1973; 83-9]).

45. There has been much debate in recent times as to what was the unique feature of hominid social life that spurred cerebral development. Theories have ranged between the hunting hypothesis to the food sharing and the mother/ infant bond hypotheses (Lewin [1991; 315-8]). There seems to be a growing consensus, however, that the real spur was the fact that the form of social life among primates, including hominids, necessitated a predictive capacity to determine each other's behavior, the basis of what I shall call in the final section: 'scenario spinning' (Johanson [1991; 270-80], Leakey [1993; 285-94]).

46. CP 5.480; 6.531; 6.475; 7.446.

47. CP 7.384.

advent of language, a new form of association was born.[48] While natural instincts are based in associations of resemblance or contiguity; language enables humans to have "distinct conceptions", which awakens in them the ability "of understanding things" (CP 7.384).[49] This ability is based in the unique form of semeiosis in which symbols (of which language is the first) are used. Peirce postulates that this unique ability to learn and use language is now inherited by every human child and is instinctive in humans, for insofar as any child "has cognitive powers, it must have *in posse* innate cognitive habits" (CP 5.504).

Symbols are unique to humans and symbols are the basis of our unique form of semeiosis or logic; but this form of semeiosis "came about for the sake of reasonableness, not reasonableness for the sake" of it; and it is this semeiosis that has enabled humans to "pass from a state of monership, and lower, to that of lordship of this globe" (CP 2.195).

5.4 Medisense and Memory

If we return now to the metaphor of the lake, Peirce notes that we must imagine that "there is a continual fall of rain upon the lake; which images the constant inflow of percepts in experience" (CP 7.553). We have seen that all the associations (instinctual, accidental, experiential and reasonable) that have been established in the mind serve to act as patterns of buoyancy and determine the scope of consciousness that will be accorded to any sensation; "for it must not be thought that an idea actually has to be brought to the surface of consciousness before it can be discerned" (CP 7.553). However, to establish the possibility of judgement, by which an abstracted idea can be compared with other ideas in memory, it would seem requisite that Peirce must also establish how it is that attention is able to discern ideas located at different depths.

This is by no means a new problem. A favorite analogy of Daniel Dennett is that of Plato's aviary: if our thoughts are like the birds in a cage, how is it that we get the right ones to fly to us at the right times (Dennett [1993; 222-5, 266, 270-80, 301])? A.J. Ayer sees that same problem in terms of the difference between 'habit-memory' and the 'memory of events' (Ayer [1961; 134, 142-8]). Habit-memories have *suggestiveness*, but memory of events need to be evoked purely from the attentive capacities of the conscious mind.

Peirce, in commenting on Fraser's edition of the works of Berkeley, does acknowledge this problem (CP 8.30). His answer to it, however, takes us back to the idea of associational habits as states of feeling. Writing for the

---

48. CP 2.280; 4.157.
49. See also CP 7.446; 7.455; 7.579.

Monist in 1892, Peirce said that the three elements of any idea are:

> The first is its intrinsic quality as a feeling. The second is
> the energy with which it affects other ideas, an energy
> which is infinite in the here-and-nowness of immediate
> sensation, finite and relative in the recency of the past.
> The third element is the tendency of an idea to bring
> along other ideas with it. (CP 6.135)

Each idea is, by nature, accompanied by a state of feeling which has the "energy" to call up other ideas. In calling up these, others are brought along with them according to the principles I have outlined in the web of associations. Peirce also often speaks about objective and subjective intensity. Perceptual facts have objective intensity, while ideas have subjective intensity or vividness. However, through the subjective intensity of attention or abstraction even subjectively weak ideas can become subjectively intense.

So attention itself is a state of feeling in the organism.[50] It has the ability to set into motion the different patterns of buoyancy which filter the upcoming ideas until the relevant one emerges to synthetic consciousness. In brief, the associations at all depths in the lake are in a constant flux upwards or downwards. Downwards, because the "mind has but a finite area at each level" and, as an associated group of ideas rise, this "inevitably involves the carrying of other ideas down" (CP 7.554).

Robert Corrington says that for "Freud, of course, unconscious material remains hidden until it can be impelled into view by indirect analytic means"; but Peirce's model is more subtle, because it is "teleological in the sense that the skeletal-sets drive toward the light of awareness" (Corrington [1993; 105]).

---

50. CP 3.158; 4.157; 7.497. Although it is true that the feeling of a mental state can never be directly studied, it is still legitimate, I believe, to assume it as a causal factor in the etiology of thought and behavior. More and more studies point very decisively to the central role played by feeling or affective states in the establishment of primary motivation, the elicitation of hereditary instincts and the development of new neural patterns in learning and adaptation (see, for example, Cicada [1965]). William Mc Dougall says that "felt excitement, accompanying the operation of any instinct, is specific in quality to that instinct ... the felt excitement is apt to be strong and of a highly specific quality in the operation of some instincts, less strong and of less specific quality in other cases" (Mc Dougall [1922; 325]). Paul Thomas Young, who quotes many studies on the feeding behavior of rats and humans, concedes that while affective processes cannot be perfectly correlated with any response or stimulus pattern, they are "however, assumed on the basis of observed behavioral development" (Young [1952; 254]). John P. Seward quotes the three characteristics of central motive states from Morgan, "the properties of perpetuating itself, evoking general activity, and "priming" and emitting specific reactions" (Seward [1952; 407]).

6. CONCLUDING REMARKS

I set myself the task to explore some of the reasons why Peirce came to be convinced that instinct was the foundation for the possibility of conscious experience and reason. This, I hope, has been accomplished. In this volume Peirce's existential graphs will be discussed. It is fitting, then, to end this paper with a few comments on how these fit into his reflections on instinct and reason. From what has preceded, it is clear that memory is the sum total of all associative habits that constitute the particular organism. Peirce is clear that instinct, if it means anything, is the inherited memory of the past growth of the species.[51] What is clear from Peirce's writings is that:

> ... the sum of it all is that our logically controlled thoughts compose a small part of the mind, the mere blossom of a vast complexus, which we may call the instinctive mind. (CP 5.212)

Instinct is that which accounts for everything in the relational potential of living forms. Peirce does not discriminate in the relational potentials between the phenotypical and the genotypical features of living forms and sees instinct as any "inborn determination of the individual's Nature" (MS 1343: 22 [1902]). I have already noted that as the operative desire (purpose) of living forms becomes more and more specific, a hierarchy of instincts grow up which enhance progressively the organism's atonement to the environment and scope of self-control. This emerging self-control is evidenced particularly in the different capacities for development and the different behavioral scalings that we witness through the various levels of living forms. If one has any doubt as to the scope of self-control in the instinctive mind of animals, for example, one could consider its prime functions:

(1)   to control and coordinate, especially in accord with sensory inputs, the neuromotor activity;

(2)   in response to particular stimuli, to set complex programs into actions which are contained in the genetically determined elements of circuity;

(3)   to refine and enrich these innate programs by registering events that are significant to the programs and to group these into classes associated by their relationship of contiguity and resemblance. (Adapted from: Monod [1974; 140])

---

51. CP 2.170; 2.181; 2.711; 5.212; 7.381; 7.498; 7.550.

Peirce is quite convinced that animals are "capable of more than one grade of self-control", but our superiority to them is evidenced in our "greater number of grades of self-control" (CP 5.533). To be able to associate and register events, an animal must have a seminal power of attention (abstraction), in fact the "interest which the uniformities of Nature have for an animal measures his place in the scale of intelligence" (CP 6.406). But humans have not only the power to associate experiences and ideas, they also have the power to consciously "*represent* and *simulate*" (Monod [1974; 140]).

> We imagine cases, place mental diagrams before our
> mind's eye, and multiply these cases, until a habit is
> formed of expecting. (CP 2.170)

This ability of diagrammatic-manipulation in the imagination or scenario-spinning comes to humans in the Medisense of attention but it is also facilitated by the free-play of the imagination (association and suggestion). In humans, instinct is always "conscious" and so human "behaviour is always partially controlled by the deliberate exercise of the imagination and reflexion" (MS 1343: 21 [1902]). In fact, says Peirce, the only difference between human reasoning and the mental process which results in instinctive judgements is "that the latter, unlike the former, is not subject to critical control" (MS 1343: 24 [1902]).[52] The free-play of the imagination is, for Peirce, the natural energy that any state of feeling has to call up others associated to it and the spontaneous chains of thought that the mind initiates. Peirce, when describing the latter, says that, in the absence of external impressions, thoughts:

> ... chase one another through the mind in a sort of Baccic
> train. Each suggests another. After a while, the clear chain
> of thought is broken, the ideas remain scattered for a time,
> and then reconcentrate in another train. (CP 7.451)

If, in this chain or *uncontrolled play* of thought, an intensely vivid combination occurs it automatically rises to the surface of the lake. Through attention and scenario-spinning, then, a person is able to expedite the formation of new associational habits and this is what establishes the accumulative capacity of people to self-criticism and self-control. Self-criticism is established precisely because the human mind is "capable of logical criticism of its beliefs"; and, so, in the progress of experience and learning, is able to adapt these beliefs more and more to how they consider

---

52. CP 3.527; 4.540; 5.440; 5.511; 7.444; 7.450.

reality (and their place therein) to be.[53] Peirce also notes that the facilities of attention and scenario-spinning are at the basis of the whole enterprise of mathematical and logical thought.[54] Vincent Colapietro sums this up as follows:

> ... self-control grows out of a hierarchy of habits; however, once this self-control emerges, there arises the possibility of having some ... formations of habits grow out of self-control. (Colapietro [1985; 495]).

Perhaps, most importantly, these facilities establish the ability to create and change symbols and so are foundational to the whole enterprise of human life.

> A Symbol incorporates a habit, and is indispensable to the application of any *intellectual* habit, *at least*. Moreover, Symbols afford the means of thinking about thoughts in ways in which we could not otherwise think of them. They enable us, for example, to create Abstractions, without which we should lack a great engine of discovery ... and in many respects they are the very warp of reason. (CP 4.531)

References

AYER, A.J. [1961] *The Problem of Knowledge*, Harmondsworth, Middlesex: Penguin Books.

AYIM, M. [1974] 'Retroduction: The Rational Instinct', in: *Transactions of the Charles S. Peirce Society* X: 34-43.

BEACH, F.A. [1955] 'The Descent of Instinct', in: *The Psychological Review* 62: 401-10.

CICADA, G.A. (ed.) [1965] *Animal Drives*, New York: D. van Nostrand.

COLAPIETRO, V.M. [1985] 'Inwardness and Autonomy: A Neglected Aspect of Peirce's Approach to Mind', in: *Transactions of the Charles S. Peirce Society* XXI: 485-512.

CORRINGTON, R.S. [1993] *An Introduction to C.S. Peirce*, Lanham, Maryland: Rowman & Littlefield.

CRAIG, W. [1918] 'Appetites and Aversions as Constituents of Instincts', in: *Biological Bulletin* 34: 91-107.

---

53. CP 7.360; see also CP 5.440; 6.286; 7.444; 7.355.
54. CP 2.170; 3.527; 4.530; 5.440; 5.579.

DENNETT, D.C. [1993] *Consciousness Explained*, Harmondsworth, Middlesex: Penguin Books.

Encyclopedia of Philosophy, 1967 ed. S.v. 'Pansychism', by Paul Edwards.

Encyclopedia of Philosophy, 1967 ed. S.v. 'Tetens'.

GOLDSMITH, T.H. [1994] *The Biological Roots of Human Behavior. Forging Links between Evolution and Behavior*, Oxford: Oxford University Press.

HEIDEGGER, M. [1968] *Kant and the Problem of Metaphysics*, trans. J. S. Churchill, Bloomington, IN: Indiana University Press.

HOUSER, N. [1983] 'Peirce's General Taxonomy of Consciousness', in: *Transactions of the Charles S. Peirce Society* XIX: 331-59.

JOHANSON, D. and J. Shreeve [1991] *Lucy's Child. The Discovery of a Human Ancestor*, Harmondsworth, Middlesex: Penguin Books.

KANT, I. [1992] *Critique of Pure Reason*, 24th ed. trans. N.K. Smith, London: Macmillan Press.

LEAKEY, R. and R. Lewin [1993] *Origins Reconsidered. In Search of What Make Us Human*, New York: Anchor Books.

LEWIN, R. [1991] *Bones of Contention. Controversies in the Search for Human Origins*, Harmondsworth, Middlesex: Penguin Books.

LORENZ, K. [1966] *On Aggression*, trans. M.K. Wilson, New York: Harcourt, Brace & World.

MARAIS, E. [1973] *The Soul of the Ape*, Harmondsworth, Middlesex: Penguin Books.

MAYR, E. [1997] *Evolution and the Diversity of Life. Selected Essays*, Cambridge MA: Harvard University Press.

MC DOUGALL, W. [1922] 'The Use and Abuse of Instinct in Social Psychology', in: *The Journal of Abnormal Psychology and Social Psychology* XVI: 285-333.

MONOD, J. [1974] *Chance and Necessity. An Essay on the National Philosophy of Modern Biology*, trans. A.A. Knopf Inc., Glasgow: Fontana Books.

RAPOSA, M.L. [1984] 'Habits and Essences', in: *Transactions of the Charles S. Peirce Society* XX: 147-67.

SEWARD, J.P. [1952] 'Introduction to a Theory of Motivation in Learning', in: *Psychological Review* 59: 405-13.

VERPLANCK, W.S. [1955] 'Since Learned Behavior is Innate, and Vice Versa, What Now?', in: *Psychological Review* 62: 139-44.

YOUNG, P.T. [1952] 'The Role of Hedonic Processes in the Organization of Behavior', in: *Psychological Review* 59: 249-62.

PEIRCE'S EXISTENTIAL GRAPHS:
FIRST INQUIRIES TOWARDS
A PROPER INTERPRETATION

RALF MÜLLER

1. INTRODUCTION: SOME FACTS AND STORIES

1.1 Some Facts

The EG (existential graphs) are a notation for logic. A small elementary set of signs serves as the basis from which a wide variety of logical systems can be derived by augmenting and partially reinterpreting the initial set of signs. Peirce calls the three standard logics derivable from his system 'alpha', 'beta', and 'gamma'. These correspond to what are called today 'sentential', 'predicate', and 'modal logic'.

Peirce introduces his system in a twofold manner. First, he provides information about the setup and interpretation of the system, the so-called conventions, and then he formulates the rules that govern the transformations of graphs. I will introduce EG by way of an example.[1]

I take a plane enclosed by a dotted line as the sheet of assertion which represents the universe of discourse shared by two persons engaged in a dialogue.

I write something on it, i.e., I claim something to be true.

The dot denotes the existence of a single individual, but otherwise undesignated object. To draw a circle means to negate all that is scribed in its enclosure.

---

1. For the full list of conventions and rules see the appendix. There, I did not set aside the so-called system alpha. Abbreviations like "R1" in the following refer to the listing of the rules in the appendix. That the system alpha is identical to sentential logic and beta to first-order predicate logic with identity has been proven in Roberts [1973].

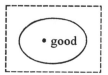

"It is not the case that something is good".

Cuts can be nested in the following way:

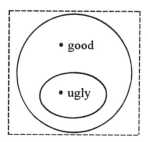

"It is not the case that something is good and that it is not the case that something is ugly"; or
"Whenever there is something good then there is something ugly".

Now you see how a graph has to be read, namely form the outside to the inside. The outer context dominates the inner context. Dots can be joined to form a line whose extremities express the identity of the objects denoted.

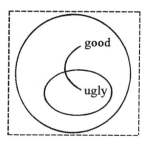

"Everything good is ugly".

Let us see how "Everything good is ugly", and "There is something that is good", yields "There is something that is ugly", in EG. I first state the two premises by writing them on the sheet of assertion.

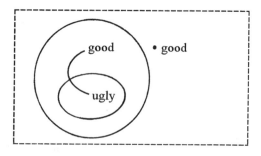

The first rule of transformation allows us to erase those parts of the line of identity that are evenly enclosed:

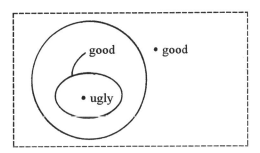

Another rule (R4b) determines that loose ends retract outwards through cuts:

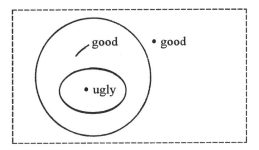

Loose ends can be omitted (R4a):

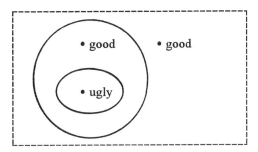

It is allowed to erase those graphs that could be the result of an iteration of graphs already present in contexts that are located further outside (R4).

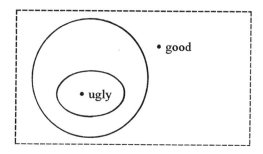

Since "• good" counts as an evenly enclosed graph it can be erased (R1).

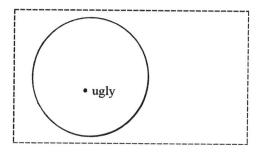

Now, we can remove the double cut (R5):

and the result reads: "There is something that is ugly".

1.2 Some Stories

My first story. It was in the mid-seventies when my younger brother one day came home from school and showed me his 'maths'. All I saw, at first, were strangely entangled circles with colored objects in the different compartments created by their intersections. "Das ist Mengenlehre", ("That is set theory") he told me. After I had inspected the examples given for a while my reaction was: "That is not mathematics. It is too easy. Can so many questions, like the intersection of the sets A and B, be answered just by looking at the drawings?"

Quine's only story. Quine first told that story in 1934 when he reviewed Vol. IV of the **Collected Papers of Charles S. Peirce**, in which he encountered the Existential Graphs (EG). But he retold the story in his 1995 paper reviewing Peirce logic:

> ... it is a cumbersome apparatus. It seems anachronistic at
> so late a date, when Peano's transparent and efficient
> notation was already inspiring Whitehead and Russell to
> embark on Principia Mathematica, and Peirce equally
> efficient notation of 'Σ' and 'Π' had long inspired
> Schröder. (Dipert [1995])[2]

My second story. Time has passed since the mid-seventies. Studying the
literature on Peirce, it is very surprising that hardly anybody has paid much
attention to Peirce own evaluation of that system. That is why Randell
Dipert (Dipert [1995; 47]) was led to claim that something like Peirce theory
of representation will surely be discovered or re-invented both for
pedagogical purposes and for research in knowledge representation, artificial
intelligence, and cognitive science. But, what Dipert had only predicted, did
actually already exist. Under the name of conceptual graphs, or knowledge
graphs, an industrious branch of research has recently evolved in artificial
intelligence (AI) based on Peirce EG. The name to mention in that field is
John Sowa.[3] So everything looks different now. I was wrong in the mid-
seventies: Graphs are mathematics. But I have good company. Quine was
wrong too: Graphs are not anachronistic at all.

Obviously, then, the following inquiries are not first in the sense that
nobody before has worked on EG. But, for methodological reasons, I will
not be chiefly concerned with the critique of earlier attempts to interpret EG.
I rather want to take you along on a kind of an expedition. We will try to
explore the terrain of Peirce graphs with a minimum of baggage. That means
we will try to get a view on that system that should be as free from
preconceived perspectives as possible. My leading questions will be: What
kind of things are the EG; and, What follows from that answer for the
interpretation of Peirce philosophy in general? I still want to consult two
sources of information about the nature of EG: Peirce himself, and some of
the more recent explorers of graphical logic. Since their interest in the EG
is not primarily philosophically motivated, I judge them as impartial
witnesses.

So the phrase 'first inquiries', in the title of my paper, has also to be
understood in the sense of being the first inquiry which will try to bring the
recent practical discussions and applications of Peirce graphs to bear on the
discussion within the philosophical community.

---

2. Dipert traces the impact of Pierce work on the development of logic.

3. See the overview of the work done in AI on conceptual graphs in Way [1994]. Sowa
began to work on conceptual graphs in 1970. He came across Peirce's EG only after 1976. In
his 1984 book he does use Peirce's transformation rules for his system of conceptual graphs and
presents Peirce as a forerunner of his project.

2. APPROACHING EG - WHAT EG ARE SUPPOSED TO BE

2.1 Recent Statements

John Sowa made excessive use of EG in his 1984 book: *Conceptual Structures. Information processing in Mind and machine*. He develops a graphical system based on EG that models the generation of cognitive structures in an agent interacting with the environment. He motivates his choice of a graphical system, over the usual Peano-Russell notation, by making the following claims:

(1)   graphs provide a more direct mapping to and from natural language;

(2)   the system allows direct extensions to modal logic and other forms that cannot be represented in first order logic;

(3)   graphs are easier to learn.

The first claim is also argued for in Harmen van den Berg's 1994 paper: 'Existential Graphs and dynamic predicate logic'. He attempts to demonstrate the superiority of both dynamic predicate logic (DPL) and EG to standard first-order logic as means of the representation of the meaning of natural language sentences. The notorious difficulties in dealing with problems of anaphoric binding of variables serves as the test case. DPL, though, still uses the Peano-Russell notation. It gains its advantage over standard first-order logic by a change of the semantics of the familiar predicate-logic formulae. Here van den Berg views EG as an even better tool than DPL, since, according to him, a change of semantics is not necessary in EG to reach the same result. I do not discuss that point here. But let me mention that even van den Berg does not seem to be convinced of the knockdown character of his argumentation because he augments it with the stress on EG's less complicated structure and easier use. Both of which are claimed without supporting evidence. Another weak point of van den Berg´s discussion is that, in the examples, where he contrasts the respective representations given of so-called donkey sentences, he only uses first-order logic without identity. Since EG comprise identity, their superiority should also be proven by a contrast with formulae of first-order logic with identity.

Another witness. The computer science department of the University of Adelaide provides a conceptual graph's workbench on the world-wide-web called: 'PEIRCE'. They understand their project as a step towards making Peirce claim true that the EG should be the logic of the future. They are attracted by the following features of EG:

(1)   the expressive power of graphical structures in representing abstract information;

(2)   the alpha and beta rules make excellent interactive proof
        tools (see the appendix);

(3)   graphs can be directly manipulated, the object of interest
        is visible and allows for rapid, reversible, incremental
        actions which replace complex command language syntax.

Barwise and Etchemendy also state that the first and third points are of
crucial importance for their 'Hyperproof Project'. Hyperproof is a system
that integrates graphical and algebraical representations of first-order logic
and is used as an introduction into logic (Barwise and Etchemendy [1996]).
Especially the possibility to manipulate the representations directly is also
mentioned by other authors as the main reason why they view graphical
systems as superb devices for pedagogical purposes.[4]

2.2 Peirce own Statements of the Character and Purpose of EG

(1)   The EG are a tool for the study of logic (MS 464: 1-64,
        68 [1903] - first part of the third draft of the third Lowell
        Lecture, 1903).

(2)   "... the central problem of logic is to say whether one
        given thought is truly, i.e., is adapted to be, a development
        of a given other or not. In other words, it is the critic of
        arguments" (CP 4.9).

(3)   EG enable us to dissect mathematical reasoning into the
        smallest steps possible (NEM 3: 405 [1903] - second
        Lowell Lecture, 1903).

(4)   EG render visible before one's eyes the operation of
        thinking *in actu* (CP 4.6).

(5)   "It is one of the chief advantages of Existential Graphs ...
        that it holds up thought to our contemplation with the
        wrong side out, as it were; showing its construction in the
        barest and plainest manner ... Accordingly, when I say that
        Existential Graphs put before us moving pictures of
        thought, I mean thought in its essence free from
        physiological and other accidents" (CP 4.7-8).

---

4. One problem that continuously arises for beginner students of logic is to understand
material implication: 'A⊃B'. In the toy inference given in the introduction, one of the premises
was a material implication (Whenever something is good it is ugly). Looking at it, one sees that
if one uses EG one right away understands that none of the two components of the conditional
are held to be true - both appear within a cut (a negative context). Usually, students first learn
'A&B'. The similar appearance of 'A&B' and 'A⊃B' in standard notations, contributes to the
difficulty reported above.

(6)   "The sheet of graphs in all its states collectively, together
             with the laws of its transformations, corresponds to and
             represents the *Mind* in its relation to its thoughts,
             considered as signs ... Thus the system of existential
             graphs is a rough and generalized diagram of the Mind"
             (CP 4. 582).

3. INTERPRETING EG [5]

3.1 Scope and Limits of EG as a Logic of Reasoning

Comparing EG to other well known logical systems the first thing one
probably notices is the particular design of the system as such. It has two
parts: the conventions, and the rules of transformation. Immediately that
reminds one of the structure of games. One has the description of what the
game is all about (to use the example of board games: the game board and
pieces) and the rules of the game (the permissible moves).

The second thing attracting attention is that the conventions comprise
more than the axioms and more than just a description of the vocabulary and
the syntax. We find a story about two parties engaged in a special sort of
activity. One party is drawing graphs and the other one is interpreting them
by applying the rules of transformation. From a technical point of view one
can justly ask and remark: What is it good for?[6] The logic isn't any different
from systems without that garment. Beta remains a good old first-order
system with identity. The particular iconic design of the system does not
depend on that story either. One could interpret a proof of a formula written
in common logical notation in a standard natural deduction system along the
same lines. Looking at the example given in the introduction to my paper,
it becomes clear what Peirce meant by saying that EG analyze reasoning
into the smallest steps possible: all the steps needed are simple iterations or
omissions of parts of the initial graph. Peirce, therefore, claimed that EG are
more analytical than other notations for logic. To that point every logician
can respond that one can attain the same result in an algebraic system, if
one, like Peirce, restricts the number of primitives, only allowing negation,
conjunction, and existential quantification.

---

5. For a comprehensive account it would, among other things, be necessary to work out
in detail the systematic place of the EG in Peirce philosophical system with the help of the
classification of the sciences. In my doctoral thesis (Müller [1995]), I take this point of
departure to explore Peirce's logic as a logic of cognition.

6. One can be reminded here of the discussion of constructivist accounts of logic a few
decades back.

Another special feature of the graphs is their iconicity. Sign and signified are alike in respect to the relations of their parts. The logical relations are mapped into spatial relations. Spots and lines stand for predicates and quantified variables. Following Peirce, Sowa or van den Berg, it is due to their iconicity that EG are easier to use than algebraical notations. If one tool is easier to use than another in doing the same kind of jobs then that should be reason enough to prefer it over the other.

In what follows, I do not want to engage in a discussion of the logical advantage of a graphical notation. Even if there was no technical (in a traditional sense) logical value to the differences, there might still be another justification for Peirce's deviation from common practice. The EG are a logical notation, a vehicle to express logical relations. Up to now we have two realms connected by a static relation: a mapping from logical into spatial form. But what about the 'processual' character of thought? Are the steps of reasoning iconically representable as Peirce claims them to be?

We saw that in EG one has one representation, one graph of which parts are deleted or to which parts are added. An inference is a sequence of such transformations. The EG are not only a visualization of thought, because that would not distinguish them from an algebraic system, but they iconically represent, they 'portray' necessary reasoning. EG model the action of inferring, they give a sequence of steps corresponding to the steps of reasoning. In modern terminology, one can talk about EG as a system of homomorphic representation, or, to put it in other words, EG mimic the dynamics of argumentation, they display 'thinking *in actu*' (see section 2.2 - citation (5)). How is this to be understood? Peirce is not giving a description of what is going on in the brain of a thinker. The admissible transformations form a set of the simplest variations possible on any graph. The logic is supposed to be normative, i.e., EG show how self-controlled thought *would* proceed. EG demonstrate that some conclusion follows from certain premises. A proof is given that the conclusion follows from the premises. So, EG exhibit only the right steps, so to speak, not steps actually taken by a thinker (see section 2.2 - citations (5) and (2)).

When Peirce says that the transformations on graphs correspond to steps in reasoning, I take it that he was not holding the narrow view that just the actual manipulations of the graphs, the insertions and omissions constitute the domain of correspondence, but that he held the more comprehensive view in which all the following steps, which one can find repeatedly in Peirce's writings, are considered as actions constituting reasoning:

(a)   Colligation (putting together of facts);
(b)   Experimentation, Observation, and Experimental Analysis;
(c)   Generalization. (CP 7.276)

But there is also a problem with the claim that EG 'represent' reasoning in the broad sense, of comprising all three steps. Neither do EG give rules, nor do they externalize how to perform the initial interpretation of the symbol in an icon and the eventual interpretation, the generalization. Strictly speaking, the graphical display itself does not account for the full range of mental activities thought by Peirce to be mirrored in EG; but the interpreter of the graphs appears to be an integral part of the total setup necessary to simulate reasoning. With Wittgenstein one could say that EG only show these elements of reasoning, or, more correctly, doing logic with EG shows these processes, they are duplicated by the activity of the interpreter. There is no analysis given in the system itself. So after all, the sequences of omissions and insertions must be the core of a 'critic of arguments', only that part seems to carry the proclaimed normative character of logic. Some thoughts on that issue will lead us into the next section of my paper. Before that let me just state that the broad picture clearly has the advantage of seemingly keeping a path open for an integration of non-necessary reasoning into the logic of EG. Abduction and Induction, *qua* forms of reasoning, share the same three steps: colligation, experimentation/observation and generalization with deduction, but the specific rules spelled out in EG for the experimentation on diagrams are not applicable to the two synthetic forms of reasoning. It remains dubious how an integration could be achieved.

These observations can be used to support another claim of mine. There are limits to a logic of cognition that are independent of the notation employed. A logical model of reasoning cannot simulate thought in the sense of giving a psychologically adequate analysis of *thinking*. Recalling quote number (3), (section 2.2), one has to state that first it is crucial for logic to dissect the process of thinking into the individual actions of thought. Second, it has to abstract from the contingencies of individual thought processes, so as to concentrate on the proper form thought or reasoning should take. Note, however, that form is understood procedurally and not geometrically. What is important is that Peirce aims at the reasoning process, the logical sequence in an argument. To use vocabulary introduced in the conventions for EG: The interpreter of graph 1 is the scribe of graph 2; or the interpretant of the first graph is the sign for the second interpretant. What appears as two separate, but neighboring, graphs are distinct moments of the same reasoning process connected by a fundamental action.

3.2 EG as a Proof of the Unity of Peirce Thought

The claim that Peirce was holding what I call the broad view can be supported by looking at his understanding of reasoning. A series of graphs represents an argument. EG make the logician an eye-witness of a successful derivation of the conclusion from the premises; but, the graphs do not do the transformations themselves.[7] It is the user who creates a graph in order to be able to reason about something that he cannot reason about directly. That means that in EG the logician reflects in her own reasoning processes the EG, so as to gain an insight into the reasoning process. It is not only the manipulating part that is essential to an analysis or representation of reasoning. In some illuminating passages, Peirce describes the three processes of reasoning by using his semeiotic vocabulary.[8] There he identifies the three mentioned actions with the three interpretants he distinguishes in his semeiotics. The immediate (or initial), the dynamic, and the eventual (or final) interpretant. Peirce holds that every semeiosis exhibits these three aspects. So reasoning cannot be thought of as being adequately analyzable by neglecting one of these components. The proper procedure of reasoning is only exhibited by the whole process of the initial diagramming and subsequent transforming and interpreting. The fact that EG are a formal correlate to the semeiotic analysis of reasoning is a first indication of the systematic and coherent character of Peirce's philosophy.

Peirce considered EG as an aid for a proof of pragmaticism. Pragmaticism is the thesis that the meaning of a concept is related to the discovery of the general habits of conduct a belief in the truth of the concept would reasonably develop.[9] One has to look at the difference that that concept would make for the existing stock of beliefs. The maxim is understood as a request to experiment in thought about what changes a concept should bring forth in the belief-set of a reasonable interpreter. Such changes are the kind of result deliberation brings about. If EG can be shown to be a model of all reasoning, no meaningful concept would escape recognition in EG and hence we could test pragmaticism.[10] Another piece that fits into the mosaic consists in Peirce's definition of a sign. Peirce notes that "it is absolutely essential to a sign that it should affect another sign" (CP 8.225 fn.10). "It [the interpretant] is created by the sign ... in its capacity of bearing the determination by the object" (CP 8.179).

---

7. Here is where we see why describing the representation of reasoning (provided within EG) by the help of the movie metaphor (as in Pape's 1995 paper) is as suggestive as it is misleading. Surely, one can imagine like George (George [1984]) to staple all the drawings of graphs needed for a particular inference together and use that stable of papers like a flipchart comic to create "moving pictures of thought" (George [1984; 5]). But something crucial will be lost then. It is the 'interactiveness'. The EG are a tool for the logician (George [1984; 1]). Their usefulness consists, to a large degree, in their property of being easy to manipulate. A logician wants to see and control the individual steps, she does not want to sit back and be entertained.

8. NEM 4: 314-8; MS 339 [1865-1909].

9. CP 6.481.

10. The above is not at all meant to do justice to the question of how Peirce conceived of the relationship of his EG to his pragmaticism. See Hookway [1985; 260]; or Roberts [1981].

A Sign is seen as a relation between three elements and an emphasis is put on the forms of influences prevailing between the different entities related. I want to sum up the above observations in the claim that the pragmatic maxim, EG and (what I cannot argue for in this paper) also the logic of inquiry can all be seen as related attempts to give partial answers to the central question of Peirce`s philosophy: How can we make our ideas clear?

Peirce's philosophy is inspired by 'how' questions, and he tries to give methods how to accomplish this and that, i.e., there are always actions or procedures at the bottom of his thinking. Peirce gives an account where experimenting in scientific research, the solving of logical problems and doing philosophy are shown to be constituted by the same fundamental processes: the generation, variation, and interpretation of diagrams.

Peirce's logical and semantical answers (as given in EG) and his pragmatic maxim make him a contemporary thinker. They can be clearly associated with what I call with van Benthem: "the dynamic trend in logic" in the last roughly twenty-five years.[11] This trend comprises work in computer science and theoretical linguistics. The dynamic trend does not only comprise approaches to semantics that focus on the action structure, but, also, theories that take a situated agent as the starting point of semantical considerations. Here, Peirce shares some of the concerns of situation theory, as Burke [1991] and also Pape [1993] rightly remark.[12]

The EG prove to be interpretable by all three dynamic models of cognition that are discussed in contemporary logic: proof, games, and programming. Right away we noticed the close resemblance of EG to games which is well recognized by the literature. The papers of Hilpinen [1982], Brock [1980] and, most recently, Burch [1995] have to be mentioned. I also pointed to the demonstrative character of the graph sequences in EG. The rules of transformation can be understood as devices to construct a proof. In Hawkins' 1975 review of Robert's book on EG, one finds them characterized as a 'Gentzen-style natural-deduction system'.[13] The

---

11. 'Cognition' has a double character: it can signify both the result and the process leading to that result. Most logicians have concentrated on the static first reading. But the recent interest in the simulation of intelligent behavior has brought about a change of focus. See van Benthem [1991] for a survey.

12. The important differences between the two approaches I worked out in my 1997 paper. For readers of German see my doctoral thesis for a more detailed discussion.

13. See also Roberts [1964]. As Luciano Floridi remarked in the discussion following my presentation of this paper at the Symposium on Peirce in Leuven, there is a striking similarity between EG and Beth tableaus. Using these one can also read off the answer to questions, e.g., if a given formula is a tautology or not. So, for the purposes of finding a proof, EG do not have any advantage over tableaus. But EG are in a more radical way iconic than tableaus, especially in that they represent identity as a continuous line. Peirce stresses that there are other demands on a logical notation than that it facilitates the drawing of inferences. It should help to study questions like: What is the nature of identity or of the material conditional? Here, Peirce claims

programming model can be found in the interpretation of EG as presented above. Programming is understood as the attempt to determine a specific reaction in the addressee of the sign. It is not difficult to see the parallel to Peirce's own understanding of reasoning as exhibited in the passages quoted above on the nature of semeiosis and argument.

4. CLOSING

4.1 Sneak Preview: Gamma Graphs

Now the time has come for confessions. I have left out a discussion of the relation of EG and mind as such, as hinted at in quote (6), (section 2.2), and of the gamma part of EG, i.e., its application to modal logic. This is not a coincidence. Only in a modal system can questions of knowledge, learning and so on be tackled in a fully satisfying manner. Again, Peirce can be shown as anticipating interpretations of modal logic that were only regained in our days. In my doctoral thesis I, for example, give a brief comparison of Peirce's intuitions and Hintikka's epistemic logic. The few writers on the topic of the gamma part of EG disagree on the question whether EG should be seen as equivalent to possible world semantics or not.[14] A vast area of research opens up in front of us. Peirce left that field largely uncultivated, at least from a formal point of view. Thoughts about the modalities, if I may allow myself the freedom to use the definite article as if there would be consensus as to what is comprised by that notion, are abundant in his writings. The contemporary logicians in artificial intelligence (like van den Berg) have presented modal logical systems based on one variant of the gamma part of EG, the so called broken-cut variant. The tinctured graphs are more or less unexplored.

In relation with the modal part, a fundamental problem arises due to the very nature of Peirce's system. It is EG's iconicity that is chiefly responsible for the claims of the system's superiority to algebraic logics and Peirce worked until his death to make the system more perfect in this respect. But he had doubts about the possibility to give an iconic account of modalities. For Peirce, the modalities are logically distinct, but epistemologically continuous. Actuality and possibility, for instance, differ in the respect that the law of excluded middle holds in the former, but not in the latter. Our experience of these two modalities, on the other hand, is not one of discrete

---

EG to be superior to algebraic notations and I would claim EG to be superior to Beth's tableaus in that respect. It has to be acknowledged that this advantage counts only as an argument in favor of EG if one accepts Peirce's view of the scope of logic, which is wider than the predominant notion in the Frege-Peano-Russell tradition.

14. Pape [(1993] vs. Morgan [1979], or Zeman [1986]. See also van den Berg [1995].

entities of any sort. Modalities cannot be conceptualized, they are lived through. If that is so, then no icon can adequately represent a modality, and Peirce said that, if no iconical representation for modalities can be found, he takes that as a proof of his view of the modalities.[15]

But, Peirce held that EG (even including the gamma part) do not yet capture all the interesting operations of thought. The possibility of error cannot be modeled within EG. I take this shortcoming to be closely related to the before discussed problem of EG's focus on necessary reasoning. Let me just mention, in passing, that I think of this as an indication of any logic's limits and as being the main obstacle for that branch of artificial intelligence called logic-AI.[16]

4.2 Concluding Remarks

Graphs in general, and EG in particular, can be seen as general notations by which different logics can be modeled. By themselves, EG do not solve any epistemological or metaphysical problems. *No* notation can make philosophical reflection superfluous.

Any further inquiry into the graphical logic and the logic of cognition of Charles Sanders Peirce should not fall short of the perspectives on EG presented in this paper.

(1)   EG is not an awkward addition to Peirce's *oeuvre*, but an integral part of his overall project.

(2)   Peirce's dynamic analysis of reasoning and his thoughts about an iconical representation of propositions, both modal and non-modal, make Peirce a valuable partner in contemporary discussions of the possibility of a logic of cognition or knowledge.

That is the kind of thing the EG are. Since Peirce's logic thus proves to be of contemporary relevance other parts of his philosophy have to be considered such as well.

APPENDIX: THE EG SYSTEM "BETA"

As usual in Peirce's work one finds several textual variants of the same subject matter. In my presentation of EG, I combine and partly shorten Peirce's own descriptions:

---

15. CP 4.553 fn.1.

16. John McCarthy might serve as the most prominent example.

Any sign which expresses in a proposition any possible state of the universe is called a **graph** or graph-replica. A replica of a graph is a token, the graph itself as expressed in the replica is a type.

Any two-dimensional surface on which graphs can be scribed is called *a sheet of assertion*.

A self-returning line is called a *cut*.

Conventions:

C1: The sheet of assertion represents the universe of discourse. It asserts what is taken to be true of that universe by two parties engaged in a dialogue, i.e., it is itself a graph. One party, the graphist, is responsible for the inscription of the original graph, the other party, the interpreter, performs the admissible transformations on the graph as presented by the graphist.

C2: Whatever is scribed on the sheet of assertion is asserted to be true of the universe represented by that sheet.

C3: Graphs scribed on different parts of the sheet of assertion are all asserted to be true.

C4: A cut severs all that it encloses from the sheet of assertion. A cut is not a graph itself, but the cut together with what is scribed on its area is a graph. The cut denies its contents. A cut with nothing scribed on its area is called the pseudograph. Every graph which is not enclosed or enclosed by an even number of cuts is called evenly enclosed. A graph enclosed by an even number of cuts is called unevenly enclosed. Two cuts cannot intersect one another. A cut which has another cut on its area is called a double cut.

C5: The scribing of a heavy dot on the sheet of assertion denotes the existence of a single individual, but otherwise undesignated object, in the universe of discourse.

C6: A heavy line, called a line of identity, shall be a graph asserting the numerical identity of the individuals denoted by its two extremities.

C7: A connection of several lines of identity claims the identity of all of the individuals denoted by its extremities. That is so even if one of the lines should be inside and another one outside of a cut. Such a line of identity will be called a ligature.

C8: Points on a cut shall be considered to lie outside the area of that cut.

Rules of Transformation:

R1: Any evenly enclosed graph and any evenly enclosed portion of a line of identity can be erased.

R2: Any graph may be scribed on any oddly enclosed area, and two lines of identity oddly enclosed on the same area may be joined.

R3: Any graph, of which already a replica is scribed on the sheet of assertion, can be iterated within the area of that replica or its nested cuts as long as that area is not part of that replica itself. Consequently: (a) a branch with a loose end may be added to any line of identity, provided that no crossing of cuts results from this addition; (b) any loose end of a ligature may be extended inwards through cuts; (c) any ligature thus extended may be joined to the corresponding ligature of an iterated instance of a graph; and (d) a cycle may be formed by joining, by inward extensions, the two loose ends that are the innermost parts of a ligature.

R4: Any graph or branch of a line of identity that could be the result of iteration may be erased.

R5: The double cut may be inserted around or removed from any graph on any area. And these transformations will not be prevented by the presence of ligatures passing from outside the outer cut to inside the inner cut.

References

BARWISE, J. and J. Etchemendy [1996] 'Visual Information and Valid Reasoning', in: G. Allwein and J. Barwise (eds.) *Logical Reasoning with Diagrams*, New York: Oxford University Press, 3-25.

BROCK, J.E. [1980] 'Peirce's Anticipation of Game-Theoretical Logic', in: M.F. Herzfeld and M.D. Lenhart (eds.) *Semiotics 1980. Proceedings of the 5th Annual Meeting of the Semiotic Society of America*, New York: 1981.

BURCH, R.W. [1991] *A Peircean Reduction Thesis. The Foundations of Topological Logic*, Lubbock, TX: Texas Tech Press.

BURCH, R.W. [1995] 'Game-Theoretical Semantics for Peirce's Existential Graphs', in: *Synthese* 99: 361-75.

BURKE, T. [1991] 'Peirce on Truth and Partiality', in: J. Barwise *et al.* (eds.) *Situation Theory and Its Application. Vol.2*, Stanford, CA: CSLI Publications, 115-46.

DIPERT, R. [1995] 'Peirce's Underestimated Place in the History of Logic', in: K.L. Ketner (ed.) *Peirce and Contemporary Thought*, New York: Fordham University Press, 32-58.

GEORGE, R. [1984] 'Taking thoughts one at a time. Peirce on linear progression of thought in reasoning', in: R. Chisholm *et al.* (eds.) *Philosophie des Geistes. Akten des 9. Internationalen Wittgenstein Symposiums*, Wien: Hölder-Pichler-Tempsky, 551-7.

HAWKINS, B. [1975] 'Review of "The Existential Graphs of Charles S. Peirce" by Don D. Roberts', in: *TCSPS* 11: 128-39.

HILPINEN, R. [1982] 'On C.S. Peirce's Theory of the Proposition: Peirce as a precursor of game-theoretical semantics', in: *Monist* 65: 182-8.

HOOKWAY, C. [1985] *Peirce*, London: Routledge and Kegan Paul.

MORGAN, C.G. [1979] 'Modality, Analogy, and Ideal Experiments According to C. S. Peirce', in: *Synthese* 41. 65-83.

MÜLLER, R. [1997] 'Peirce and Israel/Perry on the conditions of informational flow', in: I. Rauch and J.F. Carr (eds.) *Semiotics Around the World: Synthesis in Diversity. Vol. 2. Proceedings of the Fifth Congress of the International Association for Semiotic Studies*, Berlin: Mouton, 781-4.

MÜLLER, R. [1995] *Logik, Zeit und Erkennen. Zum Problem der formalen Darstellung der Dynamik und der Temporalität des Erkennens bei Charles S. Peirce, in zeitgenössischen Logiken und in der Kognitionswissenschaft.* Doctoral Dissertation for University of Mainz (Germany).

PAPE, H. [1995] 'Der Gedanke als Überblendung in der Folge der Bilder. Peirces visuelles Modell geistiger Prozesse', in: *Deutsche Zeitschrift für Philosophie* 43: 479-96.

PAPE, H. [1993] *Peirce. Semiotische Schriften Bd. 3*, Frankfurt/Main: Suhrkamp.

PEIRCE GROUP [199x] *PEIRCE - a Conceptual Graphs Workbench*, Home page of the Peirce Group at the department of computer science, University of Adelaide, http://www.cs.adelaide.edu.au/users/peirce/

QUINE, W. [1995] 'Peirce's Logic', in: K.L. Ketner (ed.) *Peirce and Contemporary Thought*, New York: Fordham University Press, 23-31.

QUINE, W. [1934] 'Review of "The Collected Papers of Charles Sanders Peirce, Vol. 4: The Simplest Mathematics"', in: *Isis* 22: 551-3.

ROBERTS, D.D. [1981] 'Peirce's Proof of Pragmaticism and his Existential Graphs', in: K.L. Ketner *et al.* (eds.) *Proceedings of the Charles S. Peirce Bicentennial International Congress*, Lubbock, TX: Texas Tech Press, 301-6.

ROBERTS, D.D. [1973] *The Existential Graphs of Charles S. Peirce*, Paris: The Hague.

ROBERTS, D.D. [1964] 'The Existential Graphs and Natural Deduction', in: E.C. Moore and R.S. Robin (eds.) *Studies in the Philosophy of Charles S. Peirce*, Amherst, MA: University of Massachusetts Press, 109-21.

SOWA, J. [1984] *Conceptual Structures: Information Processing in Mind and Machine*, New York: Addison-Wesley.

VAN BENTHEM, J. [1991] 'General Dynamics', in: *Theoretical Linguistics* 17: 159-201.

VAN DEN BERG, H. [1994] 'Existential graphs and dynamic predicate logic'. Memorandum No. 1227, University of Twente, Faculty of Applied Mathematics.

VAN DEN BERG, H. [1995] 'Modal Predicate Logics for Conceptual Graphs'. Memorandum No. 1262, University of Twente, Faculty of Applied Mathematics.

WAY, E.C. [1994] 'Conceptual Graphs - Past, Present, and Future', in: W.M. Tepfenhart, J.P. Dick and J.F. Sowa (eds.) *Conceptual Structures: Current Practices. Proceedings of the Second International Conference on Conceptual Structures*, Berlin: Springer, 11-30.

ZEMAN, J. J. [1968] 'Peirce's graphs - the continuity interpretation', in: *TCSPS* 4: 144-54.

ZEMAN, J. J. [1986] 'Peirce's Philosophy of Logic', in: *TCSPS* 20: 1-22.

SEMEIOTIC, CAUSATION,
AND SEMEIOTIC CAUSATION

MENNO HULSWIT

1. INTRODUCTION[1]

We all know that reading a beautiful poem may make us feel good, that a red light at a highway intersection may cause us to stop, that an invitation may cause some people to speak at a seminar, and that the announcement of a seminar may cause some people to visit the seminar. Thus, we all know, if we are not blinded by a metaphysical theory, that signs can bring about mental and physical effects. Thus, it would appear that signs are some sort of causes.

I deliberately used the expression 'some sort of', because it seems that in semeiosis - roughly understood as signs producing meaning - something more is involved than just efficient causation, for all the above mentioned examples of signs involve some goal directedness or teleology. The red light was intended to make us stop, the announcement of the seminar was intended to bring it about that some people would visit the seminar, and so forth.

In contemporary Peircean scholarship, it has been widely acknowledged that Peirce conceived semeiosis or sign-action as a teleological process, that is to say, as a process directed toward the complete interpretation of the sign.[2] We will explain that this applies both to deliberately created signs, such as the ones in the above mentioned examples, and to those signs that are not brought about as a means to some end, such as a thief who unwillingly leaves behind a fingerprint. In both cases, the semeiosis will ideally lead towards the complete interpretation of the sign. Thus, given the proper circumstances, the detective will be led toward the complete interpretation of the fingerprint.

If semeiosis is indeed some sort of teleological process, then it must,

1. The investigations were supported by the Foundation for Research in the Field of Philosophy and Theology, which is subsidized by the Netherlands Organization for Scientific Research (NWO). I thank Guy Debrock, Jaap van Brakel, and Michael van Heerden for their critical comments on an earlier draft.

2. See Colapietro [1989]; Hausman [1993]; Hookway [1985]; Kruse [1986, 1990]; Liszka [1996]; Pape [1993]; Ransdell [1977, 1981, 1986]; Rosenthal [1994]; Seager [1988]; Short [1981].

according to Peirce, involve a combined action of final causation, efficient causation and chance.[3] The objective of this paper, then, is to clarify the respective roles within the semeiosis of final causation, efficient causation, and chance. I will call this problem of the clarification of the role of causal concepts within semeiosis the problem of semeiotic causation.[4]

Whereas my paper will be primarily restricted to interpretating Peirce, the topics discussed in it may be relevant for contemporary philosophical discussions in such diverse fields as epistemology, the philosophy of mind, and the philosophy of causation. Near the end of the paper I will give a hint of the possible relevance of Peirce's semeiotic for the contemporary discussion of causation. The structure of my paper reflects the title: first I will give a general outline of Peirce's semeiotic; next, in the second part, I will give a brief account of Peirce's view of causation; finally, in the third part, I will discuss the problem of semeiotic causation. This is indeed a very Peircean structure, for it consists of three sections, of which the third mediates between the first and the second.

2. SEMEIOTIC

2.1 The Sign

Peirce used the term semeiotic for the theoretical refinement of our common sense idea of sign. More precisely formulated, semeiotic is:

> ... the quasi-necessary, or formal, doctrine of signs. By describing the doctrine as "quasi-necessary," or formal, I mean we observe the character of such signs as we know, and from such observations, by a process which I will not object to naming Abstraction, we are led to statements, eminently fallible, and therefore in one sense by no means necessary, as to what must be the characters of all signs used by a "scientific" intelligence, that is to say, by an intelligence capable of learning by experience. (CP 2.227)

Thus, semeiotic is the scientific study of semeiosis, or the systematic explication of the formal structure of "the general conditions of signs being signs", or the systematic study of "the necessary conditions of the transmission of meanings by signs" (CP 1.444).

---

3. See Hulswit [1996].

4. The term 'semeiotic causation' was introduced by Ransdell [1981]; though he does not formulate the problem in terms of the respective roles in semeiosis of final causation, efficient causation and chance, I think my formulation of the problem agrees with his view.

The most important formal characteristic of a sign is that it involves a three-term relationship between a *sign*, its *object*, and its *interpretant*. This relationship is irreducibly triadic, that is to say, it is not reducible to a summation of dyadic relations.[5] Though I will explain these three items shortly, it is important to realize, right from the beginning, that the interpretant is something altogether different from an interpreter, who properly speaking has no place in the formal analysis of a sign.

There is no such thing as a sign in-, and by- itself. A sign is a sign by virtue of its relation to both an object and an interpretant; *anything* may be a sign as soon as it is triadically related to an object and an interpretant. Moreover, a sign is related to its object (and to its interpretant) *in some respect*, or in respect of some *quality*. Thus, whereas the announcement of a Peirce study seminar is a sign of the intention of the persons organizing the symposium, which is the object of the sign, the information about the seminar communicated to us by means of the sign, is the interpretant. In this example, the sign, its object and its interpretant are only related in respect of some information about the Peirce seminar. The size and color of the announcement, for example, are aspects of the sign that are, to a certain extent, irrelevant. The relevant aspect, abstracted from the irrelevant physical features of the sign, Peirce sometimes calls the ground or the form of the sign.[6] However, one of the most important characteristics of sign-action is not mentioned yet: an interpretant is always also a sign which can produce a further sign, and so on *ad infinitum*. This feature is emphasized in the following definition of sign, which was written by Peirce for Baldwin's *Dictionary of Philosophy and Psychology*. A sign is:

> Anything which determines something else (its *interpret-*
> *ant*) to refer to an object to which itself refers (its *object*)
> in the same way, the interpretant becoming in turn a sign,
> and so on *ad infinitum*. (CP 2.303)

Thus, every sign involves a virtually infinite series of interpretants, each of which is, itself, a sign of the same object. The definition is interesting for yet another reason. It involves the two different perspectives from which semeiosis may be understood: a causal and a logical point of view. The causal perspective is the perspective of the sign as sign-action: to act as a sign is to determine an interpretant. The logical perspective is the perspective of the sign as 'referring to', or 'standing for', or 'representing' its object.[7]

---

5. CP 2.274.

6. CP 2.228; 1.551.

7. See Ransdell [1986; 675-84].

However, Ransdell [1986] has made it clear that, whereas expressions such as 'referring to' and 'standing for' carry only a logical sense, the word 'determines' expresses both a causal and a logical sense.

> In its logical sense, *determines* means that whatever the sign refers to must be referred to by its interpretant ... In its causal sense, *determines* means that the sign causes or produces or generates its interpretant, such that the latter in turn causes or produces an interpretant, etc., and such that, in the course of such a causal chain, there is a real tendency for the object to manifest itself. (Ransdell [1986; 683])

According to this description, semeiosis is a teleological process directed toward a complete manifestation of the object, in which the object seems to function as the final cause of the semeiosis process. Thus, if Ransdell is right, this paper will cause a series of interpretants such that, in the course of that causal chain, there is a real tendency for my intention to manifest itself. However, before examining this claim in minute detail, we must first have a better understanding of several other aspects of Peirce's semeiotic, such as his conceptions of object and interpretant.

2.2 The Object of the Sign

Peirce had a very broad understanding of what sort of entities can be objects of a sign; indeed, they can be qualities, events, facts, things, collections of things, relations, laws, and so forth.[8] There is only one decisive formal characteristic which makes an object, an object of a sign: its being represented by a sign.

Peirce made a distinction between the *dynamic* or *real* object and the *immediate* object, which are not two different existents, but two different aspects of one and the same object.[9] The object as it really is, irrespective of the way in which it is represented at a given moment, is the dynamic object. And the object as it is represented at a specific moment, is the immediate object. The former is the object as it will appear to be known when our scientific knowledge of that object is complete, and the latter is the object as it seems to be at a particular moment.

---

8. CP 2.232.

9. Consider, for example, when Peirce describes the relationship between the dynamic and the immediate object as "those characters of the Real Object which are essential to the identity of the Sign constitute an *ens rationis* called the 'Immediate Object'" (MS 793: 11).

2.3 The Interpretant

A general definition of the *interpretant* is "that which the sign produces" (CP 4.536), namely, "the "signification," or "interpretation" rather, of a sign" (CP 8.184), or "the proper significate effect of a sign" (CP 5.475). Thus, if someone beats his fist on the table (sign), to express his anger (dynamic object), our conclusion that the particular person is angry, is the *proper significant effect* of the sign, and, therefore, the interpretant. The mechanical effects of the blow are no part of the interpretant in question, because they do not signify.[10]

Peirce distinguished between three types of interpretant: the immediate, the dynamical and the final interpretant.

The *immediate* interpretant "is constituted by the range of possible interpretants of a given sign at a given time" (Ransdell [1986; 682]). Being a mere *possibility*, the immediate interpretant is indeed a property of the sign, but not a distinct event in the semeiosis process.

The *dynamic* interpretant is an actualization of the immediate interpretant: the interpretant as it actually occurs.

The *final* interpretant is the ideal interpretant toward which the semeiosis tends under favorable conditions. In the context of scientific inquiry, the final interpretant is "that which *would finally* be decided to be the true interpretation if consideration of the matter were carried so far as that an ultimate opinion were reached" (CP 8.184).

Peirce also distinguished between the emotional interpretant, the energetic interpretant, and the logical interpretant. He described the *emotional* interpretant as a *feeling* - for example, the feelings aroused by a musical performance. The *energetic* interpretant he described as an *action* - for example, the muscular effort incited by the command to 'ground arms'; and the *logical* interpretant as a *habit* or *habit-change*.[11] Whether or not this distinction is different from the immediate/dynamic/final distinction, is a matter of dispute among Peircean scholars.[12]

---

10. Only from the point of view of the (expression of the) anger, the mechanical effects are not triadically produced. See footnote 16.

11. CP 5.475-6.

12. T.L. Short has strong arguments to consider both distinctions as quite different (see Short [1996; 494-6]). Short refers to CP 5.475 in which Peirce wrote that in some case the emotional interpretant is "the only proper significate effect that the sign produces", and where he gives the appreciation of a musical performance as an example. Because this effect is *actually* produced, Short concludes that "there is no indication ... that an emotional interpretant is merely potential" (Short [1996; 495]). The emotional interpretant cannot, therefore, be identical with the immediate interpretant, which is merely potential. However, in MS 318 [1907] Peirce seems to emphasize that emotional meanings (he uses the terms 'meaning' and 'interpretant' as synonymous) are yet mere *possibilities*, which is an argument to treat both trichotomies as

In summary we could say that each sign involves a triadic relationship between a sign, its object, and its interpretant. Considered in themselves, neither the sign nor its object has any specific characteristics. Anything may become a sign, and anything may become an object of a sign. Signs and objects may be either possibilities, actualities or laws. There is only one formal requirement, which is that both sign and object are triadically related to a third term: the interpretant. The interpretant must be understood as the *respect* in which sign and object are related. Before exploring the problem of semeiotic causation in the final section, I must will first provide a general sketch of Peirce's theory of final causation.

3. FINAL CAUSATION

The most important formal characteristic of semeiosis is its irreducible triadicity. Semeiosis is, therefore, an exemplification of Thirdness. The causation involved in semeiosis is to be explicitly distinguished from what Peirce called dyadic, brute force causation:

> All dynamical action, or action of brute force, physical or psychical, either takes place between two subjects ... or at any rate is a resultant of such actions between pairs. But by "semiosis" I mean, on the contrary, an action, or influence, which is, or involves, a cooperation of *three* subjects, such as a sign, its object, and its interpretant, this tri-relative influence not being in any way resolvable into actions between pairs. (CP 5.484)

Though Peirce defined semeiosis in an implicitly causal terminology - the words 'action' and 'influence' being key words in his definition - he

---

identical. According to Peirce: "The emotional meaning corresponds to the immediate object, inasmuch as it is involved in the mere presentation of the sign. Only, it is what that presentation brings and not what it finds. It is what is conveyed strictly in the presentation itself without any reflexion, or abstraction, or analysis, or other efficient element. It is not, (to make a very fine point,) even the feeling the sign brings, since that is an actual fact, and so belongs to the existential meaning. This is only the quality of feeling. Because no analysis is involved, it is the total consciousness at the time; and for the same reason there can be no similarity between two emotional meanings. Each is *sui generis*; And the immediate meaning is, in all ways, strikingly analogous, if it be not identical with, the living personal consciousness, which likewise, be it noted, resembles nothing else. Practically, however, these extreme characteristics are enormously softened by the circumstance that we lack the mental energy which would be required to inhibit analysis, etc. So that the purest emotional meaning that we can recognize in the case of an intellectual concept is the plausible feeling of perfectly comprehending the purpose and purport of a sign, in a remarkably clear but as remarkably indistinct an idea of its implications" (MS 318: 00344-5 [1907]).

explicitly denied that the triadic action, that constitutes the semeiosis, is resolvable into dyadic, cause-effect influences. Semeiosis is irreducibly triadic. Thus, if someone beats his fist on the table (sign), to express his anger (object), our conclusion that the particular person is angry (interpretant), is triadically produced and, therefore, a semeiotic effect. The mechanical effects of the blow are not semeiotic effects, because they are the result of brute force causation.

Peirce associates triadic action with *intelligence*, because it is characterized by the anticipation of a future state. Intelligent action involves the causation of one event as a *means* to another event, which is an *end*. Thus, the action is intelligent if it is teleological, that is to say, if event A produces event B in order to bring about event C.[13]

The organization of a Peirce Seminar is a good example of intelligent action. It is so, not so much because it is about Peirce, or because it is done by some smart people. It is so because the organization of any event, even a bingo game, involves the anticipation of a future state. However, since the organization of a seminar is a very complicated business, I propose to consider the much simpler example - given by Peirce himself - of someone who has the intention of shooting a bird. Directing the gun involves final causation, but as soon as the bullet has left the rifle, there is only the blind efficient causation which in no way is concerned about its results. The bullet, for example, will not follow the bird swooping in another direction.[14]

Contrary to what is usually supposed, final causation does not involve backward causation. At the moment of the shooting, the concrete individual event of the bird's dying has not yet occurred, and could, therefore, not have influenced the shooting. The individual event of the bird's dying does not direct the shooting, but the *general purpose* of the hunter does.

While efficient causation - as abstracted from its final causational component - involves a dyadic relation between two concrete individual events or facts; final causation involves a triadic relation between the general final cause, the concrete efficient cause, and its concrete effect. The production of the *individual* effect (B), by the *individual* efficient cause (A), is determined, or mediated, by the *general* final cause (C'). The effect (B), functions as a *means* for the attainment of the *end* (C).

Peirce held the view that each act of causation involves a final component, an efficient component, and a chance component.[15] The *teleological aspect* is that each event is part of a chain of events with a definite tendency, which is determined by the final cause of the process.

---

13. CP 5.472-73.

14. CP 1.212.

15. For an extensive discussion of the relationship between final causation, efficient causation, and chance, see Hulswit [1996; 183-98]).

Schematically this may be represented as follows (Figure 1):

Figure 1: since there is no backward causation, the causation of B by A, cannot be influenced by C, but is instead determined by the *potentiality* of C' [16]

Final causes are general types that triadically determine causal processes. The *efficient aspect* is that each event or fact is caused by a previous event or fact (the efficient cause). The *chance component* is that in each event there is some aspect of irreducible novelty. Thus, as in Figure 1, each stage of the causal process involves objective chance.

In summary we could say that causation consists in a triadic relation between a concrete cause, its concrete effect, and a general final cause. Each act of causation involves an aspect of irreducible novelty or chance. We are ready now to consider the respective roles of final causation, efficient causation, and chance within semeiosis.

4. SEMEIOTIC CAUSATION

4.1 Signs and Interpretants

Whatever is produced triadically, is produced as a means toward some end. However, it would appear that signs need not be produced triadically. Smoke, for example, as an index of fire, is usually not produced by the fire in order to be recognized as such, and a portrait may function as an icon of some person on the basis of a similarity that is purely accidental.

However, whereas Peirce explicitly wrote that signs need not necessarily be triadically produced,[17] he did say that all interpretants are produced triadically: "it seems to me convenient to make the triadic production of the interpretant essential to a "sign"" (CP 5.473). T.L. Short, therefore, rightly concludes that "what is essential to all semeiosis, according to Peirce, is not

---

16. -------→ stands for a chain of efficient causation which may or may not be mediated by the same general final cause. Inasmuch as the chain of efficient causation is not determined by the general purpose that we had in view, it is still determined by some physical laws, which are final causes too. Even after the bullet has left the rifle, it conforms to a general law, the causality of which is of the order of final causation (CP 1.212).

17. The triadic production of the sign, "is not essential to the action of a sign" (CP 5.473).

the triadic production of signs, but the triadic production of their interpretants" (Short [1981; 206-7]).

Thus, our main question now is: What does it mean to say that the interpretant is triadically produced?

4.2 The Triadic Production of the Interpretant

The following passage by Ransdell (already quoted) seems a good vantage point for our discussion:

> In its causal sense, ***determines*** means that the sign causes or produces or generates its interpretant, such that the latter in turn causes or produces an interpretant, etc., and such that, in the course of such a causal chain, there is a ***real tendency*** for the object to manifest itself. (Ransdell [1986; 683])

Ransdell said, furthermore, that, whereas a real tendency always involves a three-term relationship (triadic), the production of an interpretant by a sign is in *some sense* a matter of dyadic, brute force causation. Thus, Ransdell concludes that "semiotic causation is itself telic or final causation, and it presupposes but cannot be explicated in terms of brute force causation" (Ransdell [1986; 684]). I think we may represent Ransdell's view schematically as follows (Figure 2):

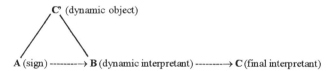

Figure 2: Ransdell's view of semeiotic causation

Thus, the sign (A), is the ***efficient cause*** of the dynamic interpretant (B), which itself is a means toward the realization of the final interpretant (C). Thus, there is a chain of efficient causation from A towards C, in which each act of causation is mediated by the object (C'), which is the ***final cause*** of the semeiotic process.

Consider, for example, Ransdell's words as quoted above; they are a sign of which my schematic representation is the dynamic interpretant, and the intended meaning by Ransdell is the dynamic object. The final interpretant would be a complete interpretation of Ransdell's intention. Whereas Ransdell's words are the efficient cause of the scheme, his intention is the final cause.

This was an example of a logical interpretant. We should inquire now if this scheme also applies to emotional and energetic interpretants. Peirce mentioned the emotions evoked by a musical performance as an example of the triadic production of an emotional interpretant, and the action evoked by an imperative command, as an example of an energetic interpretant.[18]

First, let us examine the example of a musical performance:

(I)   According to Peirce, the performance of a piece of music is an event and, at the same time, a sign of the score (object). The series of emotions evoked by the performance is the (emotional) interpretant. It is important to note that Peirce emhasized that the score is not an event, but "a complex musical idea" (MS 318: 00333 [1907]).

(2)   Thus, this example perfectly fits our scheme inasmuch as both the sign and the interpretant are concrete, individual events, and the object is a general idea (final cause). The sign - being the performance - obviously functions as an efficient cause: it really brings about an effect in the minds of the listeners. But it is not merely an efficient cause. The sign can only be a cause of the emotions because it refers to the score. Perhaps, to the untrained ear of some descendant of a different culture, the performance would be little more than dyadically produced noise, but to the ear which knows how to interpret the music, the emotions are triadically produced.

(3)   But what about the final interpretant? Perhaps, it may be understood in the following way, suggested by Short [1981; 216]: it may take several hearings for one to discover all the musical nuances. Thus, there may be a progression in successive dynamical emotional interpretants, such that in the final emotional interpretant a complete manifestation of the score would be evoked.

The second illustration is an imperative command of an officer:

(1)   The dynamic object of the command is the will of the officer, that is to say, the *type* of action that is willed by the officer. The effort of obeying the order is the energetic interpretant.[19]

---

18. CP 5.475.
19. CP 5.473; MS 318: 00034-7 [1907].

(2)   Short's suggestion [1981; 216] is to understand the final
        energetic interpretant as that effort that expresses the order
        in the best possible way.

Thus, our diverse examples of the triadic production of interpretants seem
to confirm our general scheme, according to which there is a causal chain
of events from sign to final interpretant, which is mediated by the dynamic
object, being the final cause of the process. But, of course, this is not
sufficient proof that our scheme is universally valid. I even think it is not.
Though it may provide a good insight into many semeiotic processes, there
are definitely examples in which the dynamic object is not the final cause
of the process. Consider, for example, Short's example (used by him in a
different context) of the flight of a deer elicited by a noise. The deer
interprets the noise as being a sign of a predator, which implies danger. The
goal of the deer, which is of course safety, does not coincide with the object
of the sign, which is danger (Short [1981; 207-8]).

Nevertheless, for now we will stick our heads into the sand, and continue
as if our scheme is universally valid. We can then pursue our investigation
into the role of causal concepts within semeiosis more sedately.

4.3 The Roles of Final Causation, Efficient Causation, and Chance within Semeiosis

Since we have not spoken a word yet about the role of objective chance
within semeiosis, we will start with that. In fact it is the simplest part of our
scheme. There is objective chance involved in semeiosis, inasmuch as signs
are never completely determinate and, therefore, permit a latitude of
different dynamic interpretants.[20] Thus, every sign is indeterminate to the
extent that it does not provide a complete representation of its object.[21]

However, there is another, less simple question: What do we mean by
saying that the sign is, in some sense, the efficient cause of the interpretant?
In the following passage, Peirce makes clear that, within the context of his
semeiotic, we must take the word 'causation' in a somewhat liberal sense:

> No sign can function as such except so far as it is
> interpreted in another sign ... Consequently it is absolutely
> essential to a sign that it should *affect* another sign. In
> using this causal word, "affect," I do not refer to
> invariable accompaniment or sequence, merely, or

---

20. CP 5.477.

21. A complete determinate sign would be "absolutely unconnected with any other" sign
(CP 4.583; Joswick [1996; 94]).

necessarily. What I mean is that when there is a sign there *will be* an interpretation in another sign. *The essence of the relation is in the conditional futurity*; but it is not essential that there should be absolutely no exception ... If the exceptions are, as they occur, as many or nearly as many as the cases of following the rule, the causality would be in my terminology 'very weak.' But if there is any *would-be* at all, there is more or less causation; for *that is all I mean by causation*. I do not pretend that this is an accurate analysis of the ordinary conception, or a parlance to be recommended. It is simply what I mean in this connection. It leaves the whole question of what there may be of a metaphysical character quite open. (MS 427: 00025 [1902]; italics mine)

This, indeed, would not count as an adequate representation of the received view of causality, because it involves a radically different temporal perspective. Whereas Peirce put the essence of the causal relation in the 'conditional futurity', the standard view puts it in the 'factual past': we can only talk about causes *after* the effects have occurred. If we distinguish between *causality* (as the relation between two given events) and *causation* (expressing the act of bringing about an event); then, Peirce obviously had *causation* in mind. The quoted passage makes clear that the term causation, as used by Peirce in the context of semeiotics, refers to an event or an action, namely the creation of the interpretant by the sign.[22]

Thus, rather than taking efficient causes as univocal determinants of fact, Peirce preferred to use the term in the sense that, given a *sign as a cause*, there will be a *tendency to create an interpretant*. Thus, the sign - conceived purely in its capacity of an efficient cause - only determines *that* (under favorable circumstances) an interpretant will be created, but not *what* the interpretant will be. What the interpretant will be is determined by the *form* of the sign, which is the final cause of the semeiosis, as I will try to explain presently.

Peirce defined a sign as "a Medium for the communication of a Form" (MS 793: 1). He explained that somehow a form is communicated from the object, through the sign, to the interpretant. This form, however, is neither a quality nor some existent thing, but a *general rule*:

---

22. This is also expressed by Peirce's following description of a sign: "A sign ... is anything which stands to somebody for something in some respect or capacity. It addresses somebody, that is, creates in the mind of that person an equivalent sign, or perhaps a more developed sign. That sign which it creates I call the *interpretant* of the first sign" (CP 2.228).

> That which is communicated from the Object through the
> Sign to the Interpretant is a Form; that is to say, it is
> nothing like an existent, but is a power, is the fact that
> something would happen under certain conditions. This
> Form is *really* embodied in the object, meaning that the
> conditional relation which constitutes the form is true of
> the form as it is in the object. In the sign it is embodied
> only in a *representative* sense, meaning that whether by
> virtue of some real modification of the Sign, or otherwise,
> the Sign becomes endowed with the power of communica-
> ting to an interpretant. (MS 793: 3)

Thus, the Form is a *conditional relation* of the form: if p, then q. As such, it is a general rule or final cause.

Consider the example of a military officer who uses the sign: Forward march! The object of the sign is the *type* of action that is willed by the officer. The dynamic interpretant is the soldiers moving forward. Thus, formulated in terms of a conditional statement, the object of the sign is the general rule that *if* some officer gives an order, *then* the soldiers should obey. This may be expressed in the form of a syllogism:

> Major premiss: *if* some officer says: Forward march, *then*
> the soldiers will move forward (object).
> Minor premiss: an officer says: Forward march! (sign).
>
> ───
>
> Conclusion: the   soldiers   are   moving   forward
> (interpretant).[23]

Thus, the major premiss is the general rule or the *final cause*: if the officer gives his command, then the soldiers will show a *tendency* to obey it.[24] The minor premiss is the command, which is the efficient cause. The conclusion is the *effect* brought about by the command. Conceived semeiotically, the dynamic object is the major, the sign is the minor, and the interpretant is the conclusion.

If my interpretation of the above given example is correct, then it teaches us an important lesson about the nature of final causes as such and, therefore, also about the dynamic object. The important point is that the final cause does not make the soldiers move, but the sign does.

───

23. This is another way to express Peirce's insight that "final causation is logical causati-on" (CP 1.250).

24. There may be other factors involved which prevent or hinder some soldiers in obeying the command.

We can sum up our corollaries as such:

(1)   In itself, the general rule: if *p* (forward march!), then *q* (moving forward); does nothing. It does not determine *that* an action will take place; it will only determine *what* type of action it will be, given that an action takes place. In other words: it does not determine the action *qua* action, but it determines the *form* of the action. Thus, final causes are causes in an altogether different sense than efficient causes. They are general *constraints* rather than concrete producing events.

(2)   Whereas the function of the sign is to generate an interpretant,[25] the function of the dynamic object is not to create an interpretant, but to constrain a series of interpretants. The dynamic object, which is the form of the sign, is a final cause which functions as a constraint on the semeiotic process; it in-*forms* the process to con-*form* to its original purpose or form.[26]

4.4 Some Problems

A while back, we decided to stick our heads into the sand and consider my interpretation of Peirce's view of semeiotic causation as unproblematic. I appreciate that you were willing to join me in that oppressive experience. But we had better get our heads out of the sand now, and face at least some of the problems that are involved in my analysis of Peirce's view.

First, I wish to recall the example of the fleeing deer, that does not fit into my scheme. I think it would be easy to find many analogous examples. Then, there are also some problems that I did not address: for example, I have not examined the relationship between the dynamic object and the immediate object, which, I am pretty sure, would provide a new dimension to our discussion. Thirdly, I have not given an explicit analysis of the term 'determine', which is not only a key notion in Peirce's semeiotic, but which is also of eminent importance for the study of the role of causal concepts within Peirce's conception of semeiosis. For there are a great many definitions, according to which the object is said somehow to determine the sign, and the sign is said somehow to determine the interpretant. It may suffice here to offer the hypothesis that 'determine' is a general term which, depending on the context of use, refers to either efficient causation, or final causation, or to a combined action of efficient and final causation.

---

25. CP 2.228.
26. PW 196.

However, there is one problem which bothers me most of all, and which is of a more general philosophical concern. My point is this: we have seen that the most important formal characteristic of semeiosis is its irreducible triadicity. However, there are indications that Peirce conceived of semeiosis not just as an exemplification of Thirdness; but, much more radically, that he conceived semeiosis as the only true form of Thirdness.[27] And, whereas Thirdness involves teleology, the conclusion seems justified that it was Peirce's view that all teleological or causal processes are of a semeiotic nature. But if this is correct, then we cannot but conclude that semeiotic concepts are more fundamental than causal concepts, which entails that the attempt to explicate Peirce's semeiotic in causal terms would be putting the cart before the horse. (This would entail that this whole paper has been a complicated exercise in putting the cart before the horse).

Thus, it would appear that this would change our whole outlook on the problem, because our problem itself has changed. Perhaps it would be more fruitful - and philosophically much more interesting - to reformulate our original problem of semeiotic causation. Instead of considering it as the problem of the role of causal concepts within semeiosis, we could consider it as the problem of how to analyze the concept of causation in terms of Peirce's semeiotic.

I can only give a vague idea of the direction in which that analysis might go. Our primary vantage point should be our experience that nothing is more real than the present, and that both the past and the future are abstractions derived from our experiences of concrete events. Thus our vantage point is that causation - the act of bringing about an event - is more fundamental than causality - which is the relation between two given events. And, just as "no sign can function as such except so far as it is interpreted in another sign", no event can function except so far as it brings about another event.[28]

Perhaps it would be fruitful to conceive causation as the creation of the interpretant by the sign, as mediated by the dynamic object. Causality, or cause-effect relationships, then, are the result of a process of abstraction. Whereas the primary reality is semeiosis or sign *action*, the secondary reality is the *relationship* between signs and their interpretants, which may be conceived as cause-effect relations.

Of course, I do not say that this view is unproblematic, but perhaps it may provide a new approach toward the old and tired problem of causality.

---

27. See for example CP 5.484 and PW 31.

28. MS 427 [1902].

5. CONCLUSION

The objective of my paper was to clarify the respective roles within semeiosis of final causation, efficient causation, and chance. I have called this the problem of semeiotic causation. In order to meet this objective, I have first explained some of the basic notions of Peirce's semeiotic. Then, in the second part, I have given a brief explanation of Peirce's view of causation. I have explained how each act of causation involves a final component, an efficient component, and a chance component. In the third part, I have tried to explain in what sense the dynamic object may be understood as the final cause of semeiosis. Moreover, I have tried to show in what sense the sign may be understood as the efficient cause of the interpretant, and in what sense there is objective chance involved in each stage of the semeiosis process. Finally, I have mentioned a number of problems that are involved in my analysis of Peirce's view, and I have given some speculations about a new approach to our problem, and to the problem of causation in general.

References

COLAPIETRO, V. [1989] *Peirce's Approach to the Self: A Semiotic Perspective on Human Subjectivity*, Albany: State University of New York Press.

HAUSMAN, C.R. [1993] *Charles S. Peirce's Evolutionary Philosophy*, Cambridge: Cambridge University Press.

HOOKWAY, C.J. [1985] *Peirce*, London: Routledge & Kegan Paul.

HULSWIT, M. [1996] 'Teleology: A Peircean Critique of Ernst Mayr's Theory', in: *Transactions of the Charles S. Peirce Society* XXX11: 182-214.

JOSWICK, H. [1996] 'The object of semeiotic', in: V. Colapietro and T. Olshewsky (eds.) *Peirce's Doctrine of Signs. Theory, Applications, and Connections*, Berlin: Mouton de Gruyter.

KRUSE, F. [1986] 'Indexicality and the Abductive Link', in: *Transactions of the Charles S. Peirce Society* XX11: 435-47.

KRUSE, F. [1990] 'Nature and Semiosis', in: *Transactions of the Charles S. Peirce Society* XXVI: 211-24.

LISZKA, J.J. [1996] *A General Introduction to the Semeiotic of Charles Sanders Peirce*, Bloomington, IN: Indiana University Press.

PAPE, H. [1993] 'Final Causality in Peirce's Semiotics and his Classification of the Sciences', in: *Transactions of the Charles S. Peirce Society* XX1X: 581-607.

RANSDELL, J.M. [1977] 'Some Leading Ideas of Peirce's Semiotic', in: *Semiotica* 19: 157-78.

RANSDELL, J.M. [1981] 'Semiotic Causation: a Partial Explication', in: K.L. Ketner *et al.* (eds.) *Proceedings of the C.S. Peirce Bicentennial International Congress. Texas Tech University Graduate Studies 23*, Lubbock, TX: Texas Tech University Press, 201-6.

RANSDELL, J.M. [1986] 'Peirce, Charles Sanders', in: *Encyclopedic Dictionary of Semiotics, Vol. 1*, Berlin: Mouton de Gruyter, 673-95.

ROSENTHAL, S.B. [1994] *Charles Peirce's Pragmatic Pluralism*, Albany: State University of New York Press.

SAVAN, D. [1987-1988] *An Introduction to C.S. Peirce's Full System of Semeiotic*, Monograph of the Toronto Semiotic Circle. Number 1.

SEAGER, W.E. [1988] 'Peirce's Teleological Signs', in: *Semiotica* 69: 303-14.

SHORT, T.L. [1981] 'Semeiosis and Intentionality', in: *Transactions of the Charles S. Peirce Society* XV11: 197-233.

SHORT, T.L. [1982] 'Life Among the Legisigns', in: *Transactions of the Charles S. Peirce Society* XV111: 285-310.

SHORT, T.L. [1986] 'What they said in Amsterdam: Peirce's Semiotic Today', in: *Semiotica* 60: 103-28.

SHORT, T.L. [1996] 'Interpreting Peirce's Interpretant: A Response to Lalor, Liszka, and Meyers', in: *Transactions of the Charles S. Peirce Society* XXX11: 488-541.

CREATIVE ABDUCTION IN THE DETECTIVE STORY

ELS WOUTERS

> *To me, the nature of the detection-story in the specific sense is epistemological. It is an extensive metaphor for the understanding (Verstehen), a staging of interpretation - of the hermeneutic problem, the problem of Interpreting and understanding ... It puts on stage the intellect's attempt at making the chaos of reality transparent. I have sometimes preferred the word 'detection-story', because 'detective-story' has lost its proper meaning through frequent use. Still, it is a correct term, since the novel of discovery indeed finds its ideal form with the central detecting intelligence (the detective).*

(W. Wolfgang Holdheim, Geerts [1986; 16])

1. OVERVIEW

These are the words of Holdheim that permit to sketch the context in which we shall consider Peirce's notion of abduction.[1]

We shall concentrate on the element of 'detection' in detective literature or, in other words, on the logical means used by fictional detectives in their attempt to find the solution of the problem posed by the initial crime. It will become clear that Peirce's theory of abductive inference has particular relevance to the discussion of this sort of clarification process.

---

1. Our translation of the original text: "Het wezen van het detectie-verhaal in de specifieke zin is dus voor mij epistemologisch. Het is een uitgebreide metafoor van het begrijpen (Verstehen), een enscenering van het interpreteren - van het hermeneutische probleem, het probleem van het interpreteren en het begrijpen dat ook in de wijsbegeerte sedert de 18e eeuw meer en meer in het middelpunt staat. Het ensceneert de poging van het intellect om de chaos der werkelijkheid doorzichtig te maken. Ik heb hier weleens het woord 'detectie-verhaal' gebruikt, omdat 'detective-verhaal' door het vele gebruik enigszins verzwakt is. Toch is het een juiste term, daar de roman der ontdekking inderdaad zijn ideale vorm met de centrale detectorische intelligentie (de detective) vindt".

2. The Detective's Semeiotic Activities

The detective story has often been quoted in connection with semeiotics. Several critics of the genre have recognized the close relation between this type of literature and the general theory of signs. The hero's task in the detective novel is extremely similar to the one a reader has to accomplish when he tries to understand the text he is confronted with. Both have to make an effort in order to be able to ascribe a meaning to the signs or, in other words, to interpret them. Like the reader of texts, *the detective also 'reads' the clues* that are the only tangible remains of the crime he has to investigate. In the following quotation, Heta Pyrhönen clearly summarizes this reading skill:

> The fictional detective sifts through clues, facts, and witness accounts, arranging them in order and forming a full picture of what has happened. In so doing, the detective tries out different frames of interpretation, searching for the ones which would make sense of the case. The reader is engaged in a similar operation. Thus, in detective narratives the preoccupation with narrativity is mirrored in a related feature: the reading and interpreting of stories. Critics have considered the detective as a figure for the reader, examining the methods of detection in the light of theories of reading and interpretation. (Pyrhönen [1994; 3])

What Marty Roth says with regard to this subject, referring to his colleague D.A. Miller, is rather similar:

> The activity of the analytic detective has often been identified with the 'reading' of clues: 'It is no exaggeration to say that the truth we pursue across the text is the detective's *reading* of it. For if the exemplary tool of classical detection, the magnifying glass, belongs as much to a technique of reading manuscripts and uncovering palimpsests as to criminology, this is because detective stories conceive reading and detection as fully analogous, often overlapping, at times perfectly identical activities'. (Roth [1995; 192])

To arrive eventually at the solution of the criminal puzzle, the detective has to depart from the traces that have been left at the scene of the crime. Through the semeiotic activity that consists in attaching the right value to these signs, the truth of what has happened will finally come to light.

Within Peirce's triadic subdivision of signs in relation to their objects, it is undoubtedly the *index* which occupies a major place in the context of the detective story, since it informs about its object (in this case, the murderer), without revealing too much information:

> The index asserts nothing; it only says "There!" It takes
> hold of our eyes, as it were, and forcibly directs them to
> a particular object, and there it stops. (CP 3.361)

The secret is guarded and the suspense is preserved, which is a necessary condition for the success of detective literature. That is the reason why Jacques Dubois [1992; 119] claims that the universe of the *roman policier* (detective story) is "*l'univers de l'indice*" (the universe of the index): the detective novel can only exist if there has been a crime that has left tracks. As the investigation progresses, these tracks become signs, or rather indices, which refer to the incident of the crime.[2] It is then the task of the detective to 'read' the indices and to recognize them as references to the hidden identity of the criminal:

> The concept of the clue can be initially understood as the
> apparently accidental fact - the object that seems to have
> no reason for being where and what it is ... The task of
> the detective is so to interpret and integrate the clue that,
> far from being accidental and peripheral, it will become
> the central fact of a new history. (Roth [1995; 186-7])

It is obvious that the attribution of meaning to an index can only be made possible through its interpretation by a certain person.[3] The semeiotic process can only take place if the detective examines the indexical signs very attentively, instead of simply contemplating them. After this

---

2. Peirce made a distinction between three sorts of signs, according to the relation to their objects. An *icon* or likeness is a sign that actually resembles its object, whereas an *index* is connected to its object in a natural way, without bearing a resemblance to it. A *symbol* is an abstract and general sign, which needs the application of a certain law to be related to its object. At first glance, a track left at the scene of the crime can be nothing more than a "sign" to the investigator. In the first stage, it is too early to determine whether the sign is an icon, an index or a symbol, since the nature of the connection with its object is unknown. Nicole Everaert-Desmedt describes the different levels of the interpretation of a clue (Everaert-Desmedt [1990; 97], by giving an example in the context of a comic strip (*Tintin in Tibet*).

3. According to Peirce, everything can become a sign, on condition that it enters into the semeiotic process. A sign is, thus, an entity that is always in motion, in process, since its three constituents - the sign itself (representamen), the interpretant and the object - are constantly interacting. When we often say that "meaning is attributed" to a sign, we actually refer to the recognition of the object of a sign, through the mediation of the interpretant.

observational phase, the next step is to draw the appropriate inference, which will make it possible for the sign to obtain its meaning.

3. FROM THE SIGNS TO THE INFERENCES[4]

Concerning the inferences drawn by a fictional detective during his inquiry, the traditional discussion has for a long time amounted to the following question: Does Sherlock Holmes use deduction or induction to solve his cases? When we consult the texts of Sir Arthur Conan Doyle to see what Sherlock Holmes himself claims on this matter, we observe that he insists stubbornly on his '*deductive*' skills. In the novel: *A Study in Scarlet*, the subject is discussed at length in the chapter entitled: 'The Science of Deduction'. But on further consideration, it appears that Holmes' theories are not always put into practice. Even if the famous detective calls his own methods 'deductive', there is a lot of discussion as to whether this terminology is used properly or not. In the story: *The Resident Patient*, for instance, Holmes astonishes his fans by correctly 'reading' Watson's thoughts. Afterwards he explains to his friend that he did not guess at all, but that he used deduction to interpret certain external signs, and reach a plausible conclusion. Several critics however have asserted that this statement of Holmes is not quite true. Among others, Régis Messac, author of the important work: *Le "detective novel" et l'influence de la pensée scientifique* (Messac [1975]), says that the conclusion Holmes arrived at was not the only possible one. It was in fact to a large extent due to luck that the detective arrived at the right interpretation. This is not only the case in the mind-reading passages, but also in many other situations, including those in which Holmes is engaged in the solution of a criminal case. The psychologists Johnson-Laird and Byrne share Messac's view:

> Sherlock Holmes popularized a profound misconception about deduction ... Holmes is undoubtedly reasoning, but is he making deductions? Granted that his perceptions and background knowledge are accurate, does it follow that his conclusion must be true? Of course, not ... Holmes reached a plausible conclusion but he did not make a valid deduction. (Johnson-Laird [1991; 1-2])

---

4. We find the following definition of *inference* in *The Oxford Dictionary of Philosophy*: "The process of moving from (possibly provisional) acceptance of some propositions, to the acceptance of others" [1994; 193]. In this sense, an inference is a syllogism, an argument, that is either a deduction, an induction or an abduction. But an inference is also the process that starts from an index and permits one to 'interpret' it (Eco [1984; 40], Brandt [1989; 97]). It is especially in this sense that we shall consider the term here, namely as a process of invention of an explanatory hypothesis, on the basis of a sign.

The main reason why Holmes' inferences cannot be called deductions in the opinion of a lot of logicians, is the fact that a deductive inference is defined as having a general law as its starting point, and a particular case as its end. The investigation in a detective story does not develop in such a way. On the contrary, it usually starts from the observation of a number of particular details, so that the process seems to be even exactly the opposite.

Therefore it has often been proposed to call Holmes' method '*inductive*'. This was also Régis Messac's [1975; 602] opinion, who further blamed Edgar A. Poe for being initially responsible for the confusion between the two terms. Another defender of this theory is Henri Mutrux, who refers to the procedure, often practiced by Holmes, of giving a detailed description of a person on the basis of the examination of his hat (Mutrux [1977; 132]). The situation is comparable to the one in which he can tell from the mud on someone's soles where he has been, or to the one in which he infers from a person's walking stick several details of his personal life. In all of these cases, Holmes takes the characteristic properties of an object as the starting point for his inferences. Eventually he is then able to reach a more general conclusion, so that these processes are often called inductive, in the sense of developing from case to rule.[5]

Still, there are others who claim that the logical terminology, as it is used by Sherlock Holmes, is accurate. According to Stewart, for instance, the famous detective is really deducing when he infers from the tattoo on someone's arm that this person has been in China. He says that the term deduction "can be applied to Holmes' reasoning in a perfectly legitimate sense"; but that the first premiss, which is automatically accepted as the basis of the argument, was itself arrived at through induction (Stewart [1980; 88-90]). So Holmes' argument is logically valid - it can be set out as a syllogism - but, since it is based on the premiss: All instances of this tattooing that I have encountered have been done in China, it is clear where its weakness lies. It is the first premiss that is open to question, which does not necessarily imply that Holmes' deduction is not correct.

Stewart further supports the theory that the term deduction, in Holmes' stories, is used in a broader sense than the purely logical one, so that:

> ... it would be pointless to campaign about misapplication of the term 'deduction' since it has so embedded itself in the language in its loose sense that, whatever its philosophical usage, it is now correctly used as far as everyday speech is concerned. (Stewart [1980; 94])

---

5. Although one could just as easily claim that these inferences are deductions. From general rule (the only place that one finds mud A, is in place B), and case (person C has mud A on his shoes), to conclusion (person C has been in place B).

The reason why authors like Sir Arthur Conan Doyle or Edgar A. Poe often chose the word deduction in their texts, was probably because it gave the late nineteenth century reader the impression of scientific exactitude. We must not forget that these stories were written at a time when people were elated by all sorts of new scientific inventions. They lived in a society that was largely dominated by the growing rational spirit, so that they liked to find these same ideas in the literature they read. Borrowing the expression from Thomas Narcejac, we can say that the logical terminology in the early detective literature, and more particularly the term deduction, was used in a sort of 'magical' sense (Narcejac [1975; 27]).

Umberto Eco tried to put an end to the discussion by drawing the attention to the similarities between the fictional detective's methods and Charles Peirce's '*abduction*'.[6] Since, "abduction is ... the tentative and hazardous tracing of a system of signification rules which will allow the sign to acquire its meaning" (Eco [1984; 40]), this sort of inference seems to have several features in common with the way a detective tries to integrate the indices left by the criminal in a coherent interpretation frame.

> Rereading the declarations of method by Sherlock Holmes, one discovers that, when he (and with him Conan Doyle) talks of Deduction and Observation, in effect he's thinking about an inference similar to Peirce's Abduction. (Eco [1990; 158])

It is because of abduction that the tracks left at the scene of the crime can actually start to mean something, that they can refer to the underlying truth. The detective tries to normalize certain surprising phenomena which he has not encountered before and for which there does not exist a preestablished

---

6. Confer some of the definitions Peirce proposes for abduction: "An *Abduction* is a method of forming a general prediction without any positive assurance that it will succeed either in the special case or usually, its justification being that it is the only possible hope of regulating our future conduct rationally" (CP 2.270); "All the ideas of science come to it by the way of Abduction. Abduction consists in studying facts and devising a theory to explain them" (CP 5.145); "What is good abduction? ... Its end is, through subjection to the test of experiment, to lead to the avoidance of all surprise and to the establishment of a habit of positive expectation that shall not be disappointed" (CP 5.197); "The first starting of a hypothesis and the entertaining of it, whether as a simple interrogation or with any degree of confidence, is an inferential step which I propose to call *abduction*" (CP 6.525); "Abduction ... is merely preparatory. It is the first step of scientific reasoning, an induction is the concluding step" (CP 7.218); "*abduction* ... consists in examining a mass of facts and in allowing these facts to suggest a theory. In this way we gain new ideas; but there is no force in the reasoning" (CP 8.209).

interpretation rule, by inventing a new theory that explains them.[7] Abduction being the only mode of inference to enable the invention of new laws, it is certainly the appropriate mode of reasoning in the search for the cause of a crime, on the basis of clues.[8]

One characteristic of abduction that is recognizable in the descriptions of the detective's mental occupations, is its being instinctive. As Peirce describes it:

> The abductive suggestion comes to us like a flash. It is an act of *insight*, although of extremely fallible insight. It is true that the different elements of the hypothesis were in our minds before; but it is the idea of putting together what we had never before dreamed of putting together which flashes the new suggestion before our contemplation. (CP 5.181)

Abduction is a mode of conjectural interpretation, which requires a certain amount of intuition or feeling. It is because man's mind is instinctively capable of understanding the world he lives in, that he can "guess right" (CP 2.753). Peirce calls this curious human capacity "*il lume naturale*" (CP 1.630). It is precisely this feature that makes Lucia Santaella Braga say that:

---

7. Confer Felicia E. Kruse's definition of abduction as " the process of interpreting indices in which the relation between these indices and their dynamic objects is as yet unknown" (Kruse [1986]). In addition she mentions 'detective work' as an example of this kind of reasoning process.

8. The two other modes of inference are deduction and induction. According to Peirce, *deduction* is "that mode of reasoning which examines the state of things asserted in the premises, forms a diagram of that state of things, perceives in the parts of that diagram relations not explicitly mentioned in the premises, satisfies itself by mental experiments upon the diagram that these relations would always subsist, or at least would do so in a certain proportion of cases, and concludes their necessary, or probable, truth" (CP 1.66). Elsewhere, Peirce adds that "*deduction*, or necessary reasoning ... is applicable only to an ideal state of things, or to a state of things in so far as it may conform to an ideal. It merely gives a new aspect to the premises. It consists in constructing an image or diagram in accordance with a general precept, in observing in that image certain relations of parts not explicitly laid down in the precept, and in convincing oneself that the same relations will always occur when that precept is followed out" (CP 8.209). *Induction* "is that mode of reasoning which adopts a conclusion as approximate, because it results from a method of inference which must generally lead to the truth in the long run" (CP 1.67). Peirce later specified that induction is the final step in scientific inquiry: "The third way of reasoning is *induction*, or experimental research. Its procedure is this. Abduction having suggested a theory, we employ *de*duction to deduce from that ideal theory a promiscuous variety of consequences to the effect that if we perform certain acts, we shall find ourselves confronted with certain experiences. We then proceed to try these experiments, and if the predictions of the theory are verified, we have a proportionate confidence that the experiments that remain to be tried will confirm the theory" (CP 8.209).

> ... there is something paradoxical in abduction ... There is
> something not rational in the heart of reason itself. In the
> actual midst of reasoning and thought, there is something
> sensuous ... instinctive, emotional, and divinatory ... As
> can be seen, abduction takes part synchronically in the
> nature of two apparently opposed realities. It is mental and
> at the same time sensuous. It is simultaneously thought
> and emotion. It is rational - or at least reasonable - but
> grants no satisfaction to reason. Last, but not least, it is
> inspiration, instinct; but at the same time, therein lies the
> only source of new ideas and discoveries. (Braga [1991;
> 126-7])

Still, although abduction is "very little hampered by rules", it is nevertheless a form of logical inference (CP 5.188). Various commentators on Peirce's theory of abduction have admitted that there can exist a certain confusion with regard to this paradoxical nature of abduction. Still, they all explain how the presumed *contradictio in terminis* should be solved. Referring to the original meaning of the term (*apogoge*), Douglas R. Anderson points out that abduction is "a type of reasoning which is also a lived process of thought" (Anderson [1986; 147]). Thus, Peirce "believes that abduction is logical but not that it is deductive; this is a distinction between chance and logical determinism" (Anderson [1986; 152]). In other words, insight and inference are not mutually exclusive in abduction. Since 'rational control' always plays a part in it, it cannot simply be equated with pure intuition or guessing. Thomas Kapitan shares this opinion and explains that the so-called contradiction results from the tension between instinct and control, the two indispensable constituents of abduction:[9]

> ... an inference occurs only when the reasoner exercises
> self-control in judging that the conclusion is acceptable on
> the basis of the information one began with. In itself, such
> self-control is purely 'inhibitory' and 'originates nothing'
> (CP 5.194), that is, the creative moment lies with the
> instinctive observation that given what one already knows,
> *H* will explain *C*. The correlated guess, the 'deliberate
> acceptance' (MS 451: 18), is the reasoned adoption of the
> explanatory conditional, hence, it is the result of inference.
> (Kapitan [1992; 8-9])

---

9. Analogous conclusions can be further found in the writings of Arthur W. Burks [1946; 301-6], and of C.W. Spinks [1983; 206].

The inferences used by fictional detectives when they try to solve the criminal affairs they are charged with, show this same peculiarity. Holmes and his colleagues work in a scientific way, but they still need to rely largely on their intuition.[10] On the sole basis of a few clues, they have to trace back the causes and the circumstances of the crime, which is impossible in a mere deductively demonstrable way. In other words, it is abduction that enables them to invent the solutions of their cases.

4. DIFFERENT TYPES OF DETECTIVES - DIFFERENT TYPES OF ABDUCTION

It is especially in. *The Sign of Three. Dupin, Holmes, Peirce*, that Umberto Eco and Thomas A. Sebeok (Eco [1983]) have developed the idea that there exist analogies between the reasoning methods of the detective and Peirce's abduction. But, as Heta Pyrhönen rightly observes:

> .. on the whole, *The Sign of Three* offers exciting starting points for further study. Though formulating the general principles of detection, the book surely does not exhaust its subject, if only because it concentrates solely on Poe and Doyle. (Pyrhönen [1994; 71])

When we compare the methods of the two traditional detectives Dupin and Holmes with those of several of their colleagues, it becomes clear that there are many differences between them. Not every fictional detective operates in the same manner, so their inferences cannot be labelled in the same way. As a result, if one wants to describe the methods of various fictional detectives, agreeing that they all use abduction, it seems necessary to make a distinction between different subcategories of this type of inference.

Bonfantini recognized this, and in: *La semiosi e l'abduzione*, he remarked that the abductions of Sherlock Holmes are of a quite different nature than those made by Simenon's Maigret:[11]

---

10. Here the question may rise as to what extent the work of the detective can be compared to that of a scientist.

11. Original text: "[Maigret] non confonde, come faceva invece il vecchio Holmes, le scienze dell'uomo con le scienze della natura ... Sa perfettamente di procedere come uno psicologo o uno psicanalista. Ma Maigret sa dire tante cose anche a un io filosofo. Gli dirà che le sue abduzioni, a differenza di quelle di Holmes, sono pure di terzo tipo: insomma, che sono più inventive. Anche se non si fissano in rigide matrici come le teorie, le leggi. E anche se non hanno la libertà e l'originalità delle cristallizzazioni dell'inventiva più sovrana: quella dell'arte e della poesia. Le abduzioni di Maigret sono attente narrazioni che ricercano e reinventano la verosimiglianza".

> Maigret doesn't confuse (as did, on the contrary, the old
> Holmes) the human with the natural sciences ... He knows
> perfectly well how to proceed like a psychologist or a
> psychoanalyst. But Maigret can also say many things to a
> philosopher. He will say to him that his abductions, as
> opposed to those made by Holmes, are even of the third
> type: in short, that they are more inventive. Even if they
> are not rooted in rigorous matrices, like theories or laws.
> And even if they don't have the liberty and the originality
> of the cristallisations of the most sovereign imagination:
> that of art and poetry. Maigret's abductions are attentive
> narrations which seek for and reinvent probability.
> (Bonfantini [1987; 118])

The "third type" of abduction Bonfantini mentions, is one of the three subtypes he distinguishes in the general semeiotic category of abductive inferences.

Let us first of all remark that the distinction between these different abductions was never actually made by Peirce himself, but that it was Bonfantini who introduced it. Eco, who was - as we have seen - the first to recognize the similarities between the detective's method and Peirce's abduction, borrowed this division and explained in: *Abduction in Uqbar*, that the general category of abductive inferences can be subdivided in *overcoded*, *undercoded*, and *creative* abductions (Eco [1990; 159]). On the first or overcoded level, one has to look for a 'Rule' that already exists somewhere, and that just has to be found and recognized as being the most probable in order to explain the surprising 'Result'. This happens very fast, since the Rule is almost automatically given during the interpretation of the sign. In most cases, one is not even conscious of the fact that one is drawing an inference. On the second or undercoded level, the Rule also exists, but in a different field of phenomena, which makes it harder to identify it. Finally, on the third or creative level, the Rule does not yet exist at all, and has to be really invented. In the case of Sherlock Holmes, Eco claims that "many of the so-called 'deductions' of Sherlock Holmes are instances of creative abduction" (Eco [1983; 215]).

The invention of a scenario which allows Holmes to explain certain curious facts, is accomplished by creative abduction, because there do not exist general rules indicating the cause of a crime. Different solutions are often possible and it is up to the detective to choose the right one, the one that fits all the facts. Since Eco considered Sherlock Holmes as a prototypical fictional detective, we can say that, according to him, every investigator in the detective genre uses creative abduction when he 'guesses' the right solution to the criminal puzzle. So although Eco recognized the existence of three types of abduction, when it came to detectives, he looked upon the methods of each and every one of them as examples of creative abduction in action.

Bonfantini's opinion on this matter was quite different. As we have already seen, he remarked that Holmes' inferences, in comparison with those of police commissioner Maigret, are of a far lesser degree of inventiveness. Holmes does not really 'invent' a solution; his abductions are almost always in accordance with previously known laws. When Holmes comes to certain conclusions, basing his case on a blood-stain, a thumb-mark or a tyre impression, there is no creativity required. The findings follow logically from the observed data. Maigret, on the other hand, attaches greater value to people's reactions, to their way of living and their character, which are all signs that cannot be interpreted by any fixed law. Partly also due to his 'absorbing' of atmospheres, Maigret eventually succeeds in really understanding every facet of the case and the people involved, so that he can *guess* the solution. So we agree with Bonfantini and think it can rightfully be said that if Holmes uses abductions, these are mostly of the *overcoded* type, in contrast with the ones applied by Maigret which are much more *creative*.

Since we believe that creative abduction is the subcategory that shows, more than the others, what the characteristics of abduction are (as Peirce originally defined it), I shall confine myself in what follows to those inferences made by detectives in fiction, which can unhesitatingly be called creative.

5. CREATIVE ABDUCTION

As we know, Peirce's definition of "abduction" changed over time. In his early period, he described abduction as being an "evidencing process" (Fann [1970; 9]), and a third type of syllogistic inference independent of deduction and induction. Whereas after this date, he "widened the concept of inference to include methodological process as well as evidencing process" (Fann [1970; 10]), so that abduction became the initial phase of scientific discovery. But, as K.T. Fann has remarked:

> ... the two periods by no means exhibit two distinct theories of abduction. The second position certainly represents Peirce's mature judgment on the matter, but it is the logical consequence of the earlier theory and can only be understood clearly in the light of the earlier theory. (Fann [1970; 10])

Whether abduction is considered by Peirce as a form of inference or as one of the three stages in the process of scientific inquiry, the basic feature of abduction always remains its innovatory character:

> Abduction is the process of forming an explanatory
> hypothesis. It is the only logical operation which
> introduces any new idea; for induction does nothing but
> determine a value, and deduction merely evolves the
> necessary consequences of a pure hypothesis. (CP 5.171)

In other words, in Peirce's view, ***abduction is inextricably bound up with
creativity***, since it is the essential step in the process of inventing
revolutionary theories. As Gary Shank points out:

> Peirce held that it is abduction, not induction, that is the
> source of creativity in inquiry ... Abduction is the source
> of creative rendering regarding observations, and such
> creative renderings have played key roles in the history of
> inquiry. (Shank [1987; 278-9])

If we accept this definition of abduction, it follows logically that it "is of
course abduction of the third type/subtype III that constitutes the hypothesis
assumption par excellence" (Bonfantini [1983]).

The construction of an explanatory hypothesis must necessarily be
realized thanks to the creative capacities of the investigator, who must rely
not so much on his reasoning abilities, but to a larger extent on his
intuitions. In every abduction, the researcher must, for reasons of economy
(CP 5.600), pick out the hypothesis that seems to be the most "simple", or,
as Peirce puts it, the one "composed of a few conceptions natural to our
minds" (CP 6.10). Creative abduction being the strongest form of abduction,
the chosen hypothesis must certainly be that which our "instinct" (CP 5.173)
puts forward, although this law doesn't present itself in a completely
automatic way. In other words, still more than over- and undercoded
abduction, creative abduction makes a strong plea to intuition and feeling.
The researcher has to 'sense' the right solution to the problem, because he
is forced to reason in an imaginative manner. Furthermore, it goes without
saying that the certainty of these inferences can by no means be guaranteed.
Abduction in general "merely suggests that something *may be*" (CP 5.171).
Its degree of probability is always feeble, so that control afterwards is
always required. This is certainly the case for creative abduction, since it is
the most hazardous type of the three subtypes.

6. ILLUSTRATIONS

If we want to illustrate the use of creative abduction in the detective story,
the genre offers a wide range of texts that can be taken into consideration.
Anyone who has ever read a text written by Agatha Christie, Gilbert Keith
Chesterton or Georges Simenon, will fully endorse that Miss Marple as well

as Father Brown or Maigret, are all investigators whose minds work often in an abductive way. Here we shall confine ourselves to two examples of two authors, who are perhaps a little less popular, but who are certainly rated among the most important representatives of this kind of literature.

The first author we would like to mention is Ngaio Marsh, who invented the character of chief inspector Roderick Alleyn. In the novel: *Scales of Justice*, the detective has to investigate the murder of a man called Mr. Cartarette. In trying to solve the crime, Alleyn does not set off to collect all sorts of material clues, but instead he concentrates mainly on the reactions of the people concerned in the case, in the hope of discovering the hidden relationships that exist between the suspects of the case, which could possibly throw a different light on the matter. In other words, the detective prefers not to investigate objects, but human beings, who often unconsciously reveal some 'psychological' index, that will eventually lead him to the underlying truth.

Let us see how he tries to obtain this sort of valuable information when he interrogates Syce, the prime suspect:

> '... And I believe that when Cartarette was in the Far East, you ran up against him. At Hong Kong, was it?' Alleyn improvised hopefully. ... He tried to get something more about Syce's encounters with Cartarette in Singapore but was unsuccessful. He noticed the unsteady hands, moist skin and patchy colour, and the bewildered unhappy look in the very blue eyes. (Marsh [1958; 154-5])

In addition to Syce's nervous behavior when Cartarette's name is mentioned, Alleyn finds that his reaction, when it comes to Mrs. Cartarette's marriage, is also rather strange:

> 'Well now, he [Syce] *did* get me wondering what exactly are his feelings about this lady [Mrs. Cartarette]? I mean, they seem to be old acquaintances, don't they? Miss Kettle said he made a picture of Mrs. Cartarette before she was married. And then he didn't seem to have fancied the marriage much, did he? Practically smoked when it was mentioned, he got so hot. My idea is there was something between him and her'. (Marsh [1958; 157])

It will appear in the end that in Singapore Mrs. Cartarette was indeed involved both with Syce and with Mr. Cartarette and that she finally decided to drop Syce, which was the cause of the rivalry between the two men. The woman will eventually admit this, so that Alleyn's suspicions are confirmed.

What is remarkable, is that the detective had already reached the correct conclusion, not owing to the analysis of material indices, such as, for instance, love letters, which would have easily made it possible to ascertain the amorous involvement of two persons. It was, on the contrary, the far less explicit signs of Syce's "unsteady hands, moist skin and patchy colour, and the bewildered unhappy look in the very blue eyes" that enabled Alleyn to 'sense' that there had been something going on between Syce and Mrs. Cartarette. On the sole basis of a few vague impressions, the detective invented a hypothesis that was very intuitional and could hardly be translated into the logical form of a syllogism. There exist no exact rules prescribing the conduct of a man who has something to hide, but Alleyn nevertheless concluded that this behavior was unusual. To the extent that it could be brought in connection with the motive for the murder. If one accepts the newly invented hypothesis that Syce and Mrs. Cartarette knew each other in Singapore and that they used to be lovers, the surprising phenomenon of Syce's nervous acting is no longer surprising, but can be explained. The indices that constituted the point of departure for the hypothesis being hardly positive evidence, it is obvious that Alleyn did not start his reasonings from very solid ground. Intuition took an active part in the invention of his theory. But since the detective at the end still guessed the right solution, it is clear that he did this through creative abduction.[12]

The second example is taken from the novel: *Too Many Cooks*, by Rex Stout, where the detective named Nero Wolfe is invited to have a lecture at a meeting of famous cooks. In order to show off their culinary capacities, the participants are asked to taste a number of sauces, each of which lacks one ingredient that has to be identified. This contest was taking place just before the murder occurred. Wolfe asks his assistant, Archie Goodwin, to bring him the tasting reports, so that he can see "how nearly each taster was correct" (Stout [1976; 89]). The scores are indeed very valuable clues for Wolfe:

> 'I take it that Mr. Servan has described the nature of that test to you - each sauce lacking one or another of the seasonings. We were permitted but one taste from each dish - only one! Have you any conception of the delicacy and sensitivity required? It took the highest degree of concentration and receptivity of stimuli. To detect a single false note in one of the wood winds in a symphonic passage by full orchestra would be the same. So, compare those lists. If you find that Berin and Vukcic were

---

12. "Now, that the matter of no new law can come from induction or from deduction, we have seen. It can only come from abduction; and abduction is, after all, nothing but guessing" (CP 7.219).

substantially correct - say seven or eight out of nine - they
are eliminated. Even six. No man about to kill another, or
just having done so, could possibly control his nervous
system sufficiently to perform such a feat. I assure you
this is not comedy'. (Stout [1976; 90-1])

To conclude from this kind of performance that a man is, or is not, guilty
seems rather open to criticism. It is certainly not what one would call 'hard
evidence', but Nero Wolfe still seems to attach great interest to it. The
success, or lack thereof, of the suspects is for him an important indication
of their frame of mind at the time, that can reveal their guilt or innocence.
The interpretation he accepts is the one he intuitively considers as the most
'simple', namely: someone who is about to murder another person cannot
possibly perform successfully at a test, a few moments before, or after,
committing the crime. However, this explanation did not occur to him
automatically. Since the guilt of a person cannot be logically deduced from
his score at a competition, Wolfe had to read between the lines in a more
creative way. In contrast with the situation in the previous example, the
index here is more tangible. Still, the reports do not directly indicate the
murderer. But to reveal interesting information, they have to be inventively
interpreted, which is less necessary in the case of, for instance, footprints or
thumb-marks.

The two examples we have mentioned here very briefly, are both
illustrations of the way in which creative abduction finds its embodiment in
the context of the detective novel. Confronted with a crime that can be
considered as a surprising phenomenon, the investigators in these texts have
to invent a theory which will enable them to explain and 'normalize' it. In
order to do this, they can partly fall back on their background knowledge,
their familiarity with human nature, but they have to rely almost exclusively
on their intuitions, so that the theories they finally come up with are of a
rather speculative nature.[13] There is no guarantee whatsoever that the
solution proposed is actually the correct one, which is obvious, since
otherwise it would altogether be pointless to invent a hypothesis law. So,
strictly speaking, each one of these fictional detectives is to a large extent
fallible. The reason why they are nevertheless successful, is simply because

---

13. "That which determines us, from given premisses, to draw one inference rather than
another, is some habit of mind, whether it be constitutional or acquired. The habit is good or
otherwise, according as it produces true conclusions from true premisses or not; and an
inference is regarded as valid or not, without reference to the truth or falsity of its conclusion
specially, but according as the habit which determines it is such as to produce true conclusions
in general or not. The particular habit of mind which governs this or that inference may be
formulated in a proposition whose truth depends on the validity of the inferences which the
habit determines; and such a formula is called a *guiding principle* of inference" (CP 5.367).

the author of the story doesn't want them to fail. For we must not forget that a detective story is a fictional text, and that the investigation it describes is only an imitation of a real inquiry. Because real investigations are often too boring to be told, fiction does not copy them truthfully, but only chooses those elements that are best suited for its purposes. The success of the detective is one of these elements.

7. CONCLUSION

Let us finally repeat that - as we had announced at the beginning, by quoting Holdheim - we have considered the investigative methods used by fictional detectives to discover the truth in regards to Peirce's abduction. And that from a purely epistemological point of view. We have tried to analyze the ways in which the detective hero succeeds in acquiring knowledge, so that he can eventually bring his cases to a favorable conclusion.

Every detective, whether real or invented by an author of detective fiction, is charged with the task of interpreting the clues of a criminal case, so that these can finally be understood as the elements referring to the incident of the crime. What the nature of these activities precisely is, has been the subject of a lot of discussions.

According to Umberto Eco, every fictional detective invariably uses *abductive* inferences to be able to come up with solutions to his cases. The characteristics of the investigator's reasoning that leads to the original proposal of explanatory hypotheses, are very similar to the ones generally accepted as the features of abduction. In a later article, Eco specified that it is *creative* abduction which seems to be Sherlock Holmes' favorite mode of inference, since he is often "betting against all odds ... [and] inventing only for the sake of elegance" (Eco [1983; 217]). Still, Eco confined himself to the inferences drawn by Sherlock Holmes, without taking into consideration those of Holmes' colleagues. As a consequence, he did not recognize the difference that exists between the traditional method of solution finding (as exemplified by Holmes), and the more intuitive way in which an investigator like police commissioner Maigret operates.

For it cannot be denied that the inferences drawn by Holmes or Dupin, are quite different from the ones applied by, for instance, Roderick Alleyn or Nero Wolfe. And these last two heroes are but some examples of the type of detective who relies mostly on his intuitions and whose inferences are innovatory, but, at the same time, quite fallible, so that they can rightfully be called creative abductions.

This type of abduction usually does not start from concrete material indices, nor does it ever follow previously established rules. Instead it depends on the imaginative abilities of the investigator, who has to invent the often totally unexpected solution to the criminal problem, without a really solid basis. In short, the detective who investigates in the creatively abductive way creates an original hypothesis that can throw light on the matter of the crime, whereas the other - perhaps more traditional - type of detective usually starts from some previously known rule.

Still, it would not be correct to pretend that every inference that is drawn by these investigators can invariably be called an abduction, whether creative or not. In fact, the abductive phase is only one moment within the epistemological process as a continuum. In other words, each time a detective has invented a hypothesis through *abduction*, he will necessarily have to verify if this solution is the right one, namely by first predicting certain consequences of the proposed law through *deduction*, and then testing these by *induction*.[14] The success of the inquiry depends on passing through every inferential stage.[15] What is true, however, is that the author of detective stories does not insist in the same way on every single one of these steps. Since his principal aim is to fascinate the reader, he will naturally elaborate on the actual moment of the coming up with the solution, so that the later deductive and inductive phases get pushed into the background.

In conclusion, the detective novel is undoubtedly an interesting subject of inquiry within the larger context of general epistemology, since it tells the story of how an investigator puts into practice certain methods and strategies of knowledge.

In order to describe these strategies, the concept of 'inference' as it is defined by Peirce is very suitable, since within his theory, the term is no longer a synonym of either induction or deduction. According to Peirce, and here we refer to what Gérard Deledalle says on this matter:[16]

> ... we are not predetermined to the dual straight-jacket of the imperialism of the facts and the imperialism of the laws. To think, that is to seek, to 'inquire into', to explore, to believe that one has found and to 'pretend' for a while, before starting over this 'search' for the truth, which Peirce qualifies as 'fallibilistic'. (Deledalle [1990; 78])

In other words, Peirce does not consider inferences as purely logical

---

14. Confer CP 6.468-73.

15. When it comes to these three stages of inquiry, the investigation of the detective and that of the scientist seem to run parallel to each other.

16. Our translation of the original text: "Selon lui, nous ne sommes pas voués au double carcan de l'impérialisme des faits et de l'impérialisme des lois. Penser, c'est chercher, c'est 'enquêter', tâtonner, croire que l'on a trouvé et faire 'comme si' pour un temps, avant de recommencer cette 'quête' de la vérité que Peirce qualifie de 'faillibiliste'".

syllogisms, but as triadic epistemological processes, within which abduction occupies an essential place, as the first moment of the hazardous invention of a new hypothesis. And that is precisely what we have tried to illustrate by referring to the particular situation of the detective in the detective story.

But we must remark once again that we are examining *fictional* texts, and that detective stories are never accurate reproductions of investigations in real life. It is because the world of detective fiction is presented as rather a *deterministic* whole, that the detective's inferences often seem more obvious that they would in everyday life. Whereas in real life it would take a lot of imagination to come up with certain hypotheses we find in stories, these same theories seem rather evident in the fictional context, since even there human behavior is determined by general laws (effect-cause relations). Consequently, the detective can operate in a way real scientists can only dream of. Although fictional detectives are concerned with *particular* cases, each of their problems can be considered as the necessary effect of a certain cause and can finally be translated into a *general* law. Every strange phenomenon can be actually explained, which is in fact the ideal of the scientist. In sum, just like the scientist, the fictional investigator aims at the discovery of general laws, more particularly of laws of human criminal behavior, a goal that could never be achieved fully in life.

Let us, therefore, end by quoting Champigny, who rightly emphasizes the difference between a fictional and a real detective.

> ... the mystery in a mystery story ... looks like a cognitive problem. But the way fiction uses rules of individuation is purely semantic, not cognitive ... The epistemological significance of mystery stories is not to be denied. But to a great extent it should be viewed in a negative perspective. The same could be said about the significance of any esthetic experience compared to practical existence. Analogies, however realistic they may be, must not blind us to radical differences. Basically, art represents practical reality as it is not. It turns failures of comprehension into comprehension. (Champigny [1977; 19])

References

ANDERSON, D.R. [1986] 'The Evolution of Peirce's Concept of Abduction', in: *Transactions of the Charles S. Peirce Society* XXII: 145-64.

BONFANTINI, M.A. [1983] 'Abduction, A Priori Brain: for a Research Program', in: *Versus* 34: 3-11.

BONFANTINI, M.A. [1987] *La semiosi e l'abduzione*, Milano: Bompiani.

BRAGA, L.S. [1991] 'Instinct, logic, or the logic of instinct?', in: *Semiotica* 83: 123-41.

BRANDT, P. [1989] 'Signe et inférence', in: *Versus* 54: 99-109.

BURKS, A.W. [1946] 'Peirce's theory of abduction', in: *Philosophy of Science* 13: 301-6.

CHAMPIGNY, R. [1977] *What Will Have Happened: A philosophical and technical essay on mystery stories*, Bloomington, IN: Indiana University Press.

DELEDALLE, G. [1990] *Lire Peirce Aujourd'hui*, Bruxelles: De Boeck-Wesmael.

DUBOIS, J. [1992] *Le texte à l'oeuvre. Le roman policier ou la modernité*, Paris: Nathan.

ECO, U. and T.A. Sebeok (eds.) [1983] *The Sign of Three. Dupin, Holmes, Peirce*, Bloomington, IN: Indiana University Press.

ECO, U. [1984] 'Abduction and inferential nature of signs', in: *Semiotics and the philosophy of language*, London: MacMillan Press.

ECO, U. [1990] 'Abduction in Uqbar', in: *The limits of interpretation*, Bloomington, IN: Indiana University Press.

EVERAERT-DESMEDT, N. [1990] *Le processus interprétatif. Introduction à la sémiotique de Charles S. Peirce*, Liège: Pierre Mardaga.

FANN, K.T. [1970] *Peirce's theory of abduction*, The Hague: Martinus Nijhoff.

GEERTS, W., and W. Gobbers (eds.) [1986] *Reflecties over het Detectieverhaal; Schleiermacher en de hermeneutische traditie. Inaugurele lezingen. Antwerpen, U.I.A. Internationale Francqui-leestoel, 1985-86*, Antwerp: U.I.A.

JOHNSON-LAIRD P.N. and R.M.J. Byrne [1991] 'Deduction', in: *Essays in Cognitive Psychology*, Hove and London: Lawrence Erlbaum Associates.

KAPITAN, T. [1992] 'Peirce and the autonomy of abductive reasoning', in: *Erkenntnis* 37: 1-26.

KRUSE, F.E. [1986] 'Indexicality and the Abductive Link', in: *Transactions of the Charles S. Peirce Society* XXII: 435-47.

MARSH, N. [1958] *Scales of Justice*, Glasgow: Collins/ Fontana Books.

MESSAC, R. [1975] *Le "detective novel" et l'influence de la pensée scientifique*, Geneva: Slatkine Reprints.

MUTRUX, H. [1977] *Sherlock Holmes: roi des tricheurs*, Paris: La pensée universelle.

NARCEJAC, T. [1975] *Une machine à lire: le roman policier*, Paris: Denoël/Gonthier.

PYRHÖNEN, H. [1994] *Murder from an Academic Angle: An Introduction to the Study of the Detective Narrative*, Columbia: Camden House.

ROTH, M. [1995] *Foul and Fair Play: reading Genre in Classic Detective Fiction*, Athens & London: The University of Georgia Press.

SHANK, G. [1987] 'Abductive strategies in educational research', in: *The American Journal of Semiotics* 5: 275-90.

SPINKS, C.W. [1983] 'Peirce's demon abduction: or how to charm the truth out of a quark', in: *The American Journal of Semiotics* 2: 195-208.

STEWART, R.F. [1980] ... *And Always a Detective: Chapters on the History of detective Fiction*, London: North Pomfret, David & Charles.

STOUT, R. [1976] *Too Many Cooks*, New York & London: Garland Publishing Inc.

The Oxford Dictionary of Philosophy [1994], Oxford: Oxford University Press.

PEIRCE, THEOLOGIAN

GÉRARD DELEDALLE

1. INTRODUCTION

Peirce was born a Unitarian. Unitarians believe that only God the Father
is God; Jesus, the Son of God, and the Holy Spirit are the first among the
creatures. One of Peirce's fellow-students at Harvard, Charles Fay, had a
sister Harriet Melusina who not only had become an Episcopalian and
consequently a trinitarian, but was a kind of American 'suffragette', a
feminist who had advanced a conception of the Trinity in which the Holy
Spirit represented the 'woman' in the triune Divinity:

> A Divine Eternal Trinity of Father, Mother and Only Son
> - the 'Mother' being veiled throughout the Scriptures
> under the terms 'The Spirit', 'Wisdom', 'The Holy Ghost',
> 'The Comforter' and 'The Woman clothed with the sun
> and crowned with the stars and with the moon under her
> feet'. (Fisch [1982; xxxi])

Charles S. Peirce married Melusina in the Episcopalian church and
adopted Melusina's triune conception of God:

> Here, therefore, we have a divine trinity of the object,
> interpretant, and ground ... In many respects, this trinity
> agrees with the Christian trinity ... The interpretant is
> evidently the Divine *Logos* or word; and if our former
> guess that a Reference to an interpretant is Paternity be
> right, this would be also the son *of* God. The *ground*,
> being that partaking of which is requisite to any
> communication with the Symbol, corresponds in its
> function to the Holy Spirit. (W1: 503)

Peirce gave later in 1907, although he had been separated from Melusina
for more than thirty years, an even more feminine conception: "A Sign
mediates between its *Object* and its *Meaning* ... Object the father, sign the
mother of meaning" (Fisch [1982; xxxii]).[1]

---

1. That is, according to Max Fisch, of their son, the interpretant.

2. DOES GOD EXIST ?

The question was dealt with by Peirce in a convincing paper published in the ***Hibbert Journal*** in 1908, under the title: 'A Neglected Argument for the Reality of God'. Peirce's positive answer has a very important consequence. It proves, or rather shows, that answering the question is possible on the sole condition that God is triune.

Peirce's way to God is not argumentative, nor historical, it is a sheer wandering of the mind in the universe of Firstness through 'musement'. Musement is a 'pure play' of the mind. "Pure Play has no rules, except this very law of liberty. It bloweth where it listeth. It has no purpose, unless recreation" (CP 6.458). For Peirce it takes on many forms: "aesthetic contemplation", "castle-building", or that form "of considering some wonder on one of the [three] Universes, or some connection between two of the three, with speculation concerning its cause", which is properly speaking the musement which "will flower into the N.A. [neglected argument]" (CP 6.458).

Peirce was not only born a Unitarian, he was born a empiricist. Historically, Peirce was first, from 1851 to 1867, an out-and-out empiricist and thus a nominalist: only seconds - concrete individual existents - were real. Reality and existence were then synonymous. In 1857, he wrote that "Reality [refers] to the existence of the object itself" (W1: 18).

From 1867 onwards, more precisely during the winter of 1867-1868, in an unpublished item in which he criticized positivism, Peirce distinguished between existence and reality. What is real is "that which is independently of our belief and which could be properly inferred by the most thorough discussion of the sum of all impressions of sense whatever" (W2: 127).

It will be remarked that this kind of reality, although general, is a sort of classical third, since it appears as the generalization of seconds. It was not before the logic of relatives and the new methodology that thirds were no longer abstractions, but operative rules, *a priori* empty, of the type: if p, then q.

It was not until much later, about 1890, that Peirce conceded that firsts are also real. In 1891, he wrote that "in the beginning ... there was a chaos of impersonalized feeling, which being without connection or regularity would properly be without existence". However, this "feeling, sporting here and there in pure arbitrariness, would have started the germ of a generalizing tendency" (CP 6.33). How to interpret the reality of firsts is not easy. If we say that they are *in potentia*, how can they be entirely without existence? If they are not *in potentia*, they must be a general without a **ground**. This is contrary to Thirdness, which is a rule expressing the logical relation between 'arguments', such as p and q. Thus there must be another kind of general. This generality is something 'vague' and underdetermined, which can only be 'realized' by sheer chance. One of the best commentators on Peirce (who, with Paul Weiss, edited the **Collected Papers** of Peirce), Charles Hartshorne, insisted on this point in a chapter of his book: **The Logic of Perfection**, entitled: 'Ten Ontological or Model Proofs for God's Existence'. Since, perfection is not a state, Hartshorne argues, an *actus purus*, but a destiny, then perfection is perfectibility:

> The absolute infinity of the divine potentiality might also be called its *coincidence with possibility as such*. (Perhaps "coextensiveness" with possibility would be more accurate.) To be possible is to be a possible object of divine knowing. But it immediately follows that one thing is not possible - the non-existence of the divine knower. For no subject can have knowledge of the fact of its own non-existence, certainly not perfect, infallible knowledge. Thus either the non-existence of the perfect knower is impossible, or there is one possibility whose actualization the perfect knower could not know. But the second case contradicts the definition of perfection through the coincidence of "possible" and "possible for God." (Hartshorne [1962; 38])

As, on the other hand, according to model logic, to say that '*p* is possible', is to say that 'necessarily *p* is possible'; and to say that 'it is possible that *p* is necessary', is to say that 'necessarily *p* is necessary'. The ontological argument is valid and God is real, in the Peircean sense, that is to say: God as triune (Father, Son and Holy Spirit) 'exists'.[2]

The 'reality' which Peirce has in mind when he speaks of the reality of God, is the reality of Firstness. But it is not enough to oppose 'reality' as first, and 'existence' as second, because there are not two but three universes of experience which are not separate universes, but fundamental modalities of Being. Firstness or the mode of Being as 'felt', is more than a simple 'feeling': it tends to get united with other 'feelings' in time and space, in

---

2. We are summarizing here Hartshorne's complete logical argumentation: "To squeeze this modal complexity into the mere dichotomy, "existent versus non-existent," is to fail to discuss what Anselm was talking about. He repeatedly expressed the principle that "contingently-existing perfect thing" is contradictory in the same way as "non-existing perfect thing." However, since what is not exemplified in truth is certainly not necessarily exemplified ($\sim p \rightarrow \sim Np$), and since what is not necessary could not be necessary ($\sim Np \rightarrow N \sim Np$), to exclude contingency (this exclusion being the main point of the Argument) is to exclude factual non-existence as well as merely factual existence, leaving as the only status which the idea of perfection can have (supposing it not meaningless or contradictory), that of necessary exemplification in reality; and it then, by the principle $Np \rightarrow p$, "the necessarily true is true," becomes contradictory to deny that perfection is exemplified. (Here, and throughout, we use the arrow sign for strict, not material implication.)" (Hartshorne [1962; 50]).

other words to 'exist' *hic et nunc*. Existing *hic et nunc*, is the mode of being of Secondness. The interactions of feelings give birth in the long run to a third mode of Being: Thirdness which includes habits and laws.

The first universe is that of Possibility; "the second Universe is that of the Brute Actuality of things and facts"; and the third universe is that of the Sign, "not the mere body of the Sign", but "the Sign's soul, which has its Being in its power of serving as intermediary between its Object and a Mind" (CP 6.455).

Which 'reality' is the reality of God ? It is the reality of Firstness which can be reached through the action of the mind which Peirce calls musement. The play of musement is neither the play of deduction (Thirdness), nor the play of induction (Secondness), but the play of retroduction or rather abduction. It is only musement, the play of Firstness, which can reveal the reality of God. Not the existence of God, because 'existence' can be shown only through induction. Nor the reality of God as Holy Spirit, which can be proved only through deduction. Consequently, Peirce's answer to the question of the existence, or rather reality, of God implies that God is triune: God the Father has the reality of Firstness (he 'is', but does not exist); while God the Son, although also real as first, did exist as second in the person of Jesus; as to the reality of God as third or organizer of the world, it is personified in the Holy Spirit.

To conclude this first part of my paper, I should like to insist on the originality of Peirce's argument. It is the first argument ever founded on the category of possibility whose argumentative *scientific* expression is neither induction (on which all the proofs of the existence of God rest), nor *a priori* deduction. The latter is very often used by metaphysicians since Saint Anselm, and it leads to God's reality, but a reality which implies 'existence', which is a terminological contradiction denounced by Peirce and Duns Scotus. Rather, Peirce's argument rests on retroduction or abduction, the only argument which can 'show' the reality of God without imposing on God the *haecceity* of existence. A conception which is not incompatible with God's incarnation as second in the historical existence of Jesus Christ, nor with the reality of God as first through the mediation as third of the Holy Spirit.

3. PEIRCE'S TRIAD AND THE MYSTERY OF THE TRINITY

3.1 Origins of the Ideas

Peirce was not interested in the mystery of the trinity of God, proper. The reason why I feel it is necessary to delve deeper into this problem is, on the one hand, when I read Peirce, I am continually surprised that he had experienced and dealt with the same problem of the unicity of God and God's triune nature, but that, on the other hand, Peirce's position was closer to the eastern church's interpretation of the Councils, that the western one.

The word Trinity was proposed initially by Theophilus of Antioch about 180 AD, as a synonym for the word 'triad', in the course of a theological dispute. It was also in a theological context that Peirce exposed his triadic theory for the first time, in 1866, at the end of the eleventh Lowell Lecture. I have already quoted this passage, but it should be noted that Peirce uses the word "symbol" and not "sign":

> The interpretant is evidently the Divine *Logos* or word; and if our former guess that a Reference to an interpretant is Paternity be right, this would be also the son *of* God. The *ground*, being that partaking of which is requisite to any communication with the Symbol, corresponds in its function to the Holy Spirit. (W1: 503)

Paradoxically enough, Peirce's conception of God as a hierarchical tri-unity, is better understood when it is read in the context of the history of the quarrels around the mystery of the Trinity whose reasons for disagreement are not the mystery itself, but:

(1)   the interference of the political power;

(2)   the different (eastern or western) mental representations of the concepts;

(3)   with their political implications, the two latter both partially due to (4);

(4)   the language used, Greek or Latin.

3.2 Political Interference

The first council which met in 325 a.d. at Nicea (Iznik in Turkey), was summoned by the emperor Constantine who presided over it. In accordance with the emperor's wishes, the council pronounced the condemnation of Arianism. Arius, a priest of Alexandria (c.280 - c.336), had taught that the divine persons cannot be equal, nor assimilated: the Father, un-created and un-engendered cannot communicate with the world, the Son engendered for all eternity is the ordinator of the world in lieu of the λόγος or divine power. The Son is subordinate and inferior to the Father. The council decided that the Son was consubstantial (ὁμοούσιος) with the Father (homo meaning 'same', and ousia 'substance'), hence: Jesus Christ is the Son of God, engendered and not created, consubstantial with the Father.

Soon disagreements appeared concerning the synonymity of *consubtantialis* (consubstantial) and ὁμοούσιος as we shall see. As the emperor Constantius II (317-361) was against the consubstantiality of the Son with the Father, the Councils of Rimini (west) and Seleuciae (East) condemned the western interpretation, because such was the order of the Emperor.

When Constantius II died in 331 a.d., the new emperor, Julian the Apostate, who was to write the treatise: *Adversus Christianos*, reestablished the freedom of speech and discussion in matters of religion which had been prohibited by Constantius II. After Julian's death, the Council of Constantinople, summoned in 381 a.d. by Theodosius I (c. 346-395), the last emperor of the eastern and western empire (374-395), put a temporary stop to the discussion by confirming the doctrine proclaimed by the Council of Nicea.

3.3 Definitions and Representations

Definitions of dogmas *without representations* raise only problems of formal coherence, but no difficulties of adhesion if they are coherent. To believe in a dogma is another problem, because to believe is to believe in the representation one makes of it. It must be remembered that, on dualistic principles, Euclidean geometry does not require, any more than does the Trinity, a figured representation, but that non-Euclidean geometries have their point of departure in a criticism of the representation of Euclidean geometry. All philosophers, however, from Plato (who made use of myths) to Peirce (who used diagrams and existential graphs), have 'illustrated' their discourse.

The problem arises when a same definition leads to different representations. Which is what happened when Constantine tried to unify christian doctrine. If Christianity had no difficulty in agreeing on the formal definition of the Trinity, the eastern and western churches were in disagreement about the representations they made of it. By 'formal definition' I mean, as in plain English: the unity of God in three persons, Father, Son and Holy Spirit. By 'representation' I mean the 'image' in every sense of the word: the *mental* image and the *corporeal* image. The mental image refers to the *values* given to the terms, implicit or implicit, of the definition: in this case, the way in which the unity (of God) is divided into three. The corporeal image was to be at the center of the quarrel about images which broke out at the beginning of the eighth century. In both cases, it appears clearly that, although it is true that one cannot think without images, thought unites, while images divide.

The quarrel concerning the filiation of the Holy Spirit from the Father *and the Son* (the quarrel of the *filioque* clause in the western creed) between Rome and Constantinople, has its root in the doctrine of the ὅμοούσιος character of the Son which did not satisfy the eastern church. If it is true that, for Philo (Alexandria, 13 b.c.-54 a.d.), ὁμοούσιος really meant what the council had intended it to mean, the word was associated in the κοινή with the idea of metal. The word ὁμοούσιος was used only to mean that, for instance, two pieces of gold jewelry were of the same kind of material or substance. The word had thus a material and concrete implication which could not be fitting in speaking of God. The western representatives had not the same *interpretants* and consequently were ready to accept the word and the doctrine.

Eusebius of Caesarea (today in Israel) (265-340) reformulated the doctrine without using the word ὁμοούσιος: "The Father is the beginning of the Son who takes his divinity from Him. There is thus only one God without beginning and unengendered. As to the Son, he is the image of the only true God, He alone who is God by Himself". But this was only coming back to the *subordinationism* of Arius, for whom in fact Eusebius had some sympathy. Besides, it did not eliminate completely the 'ὁμοούσιος' character which reappeared in the idea of *image* inseparable from the idea of *resemblance*.

The eastern churches found still other ways of avoiding the word ὁμοούσιος. The first was to reject any resemblance between the Father and the Son; this was what Aethius and his disciple Eunone proposed. The second one was to accept a certain resemblance while affirming the inequality of the divine persons or, in other words, to use the Greek term, by maintaining the thesis of the *anomeism* of the persons (ἀνόμοιος meaning 'unlike').

After Julian's death, at Antioch, Aetius and Eunone renewed the philosophical reflection on the Trinity. As it was the essence of God to be unengendered, only the Father was God and thus the Son was fundamentally dissimilar (ἀνόμοιος) from the Father. Whence a hierarchised conception of the Trinity which was very well exposed by Eunone: The essence of God unengendered (ἀγεννησια), which is by definition incommunicable, cannot have been communicated by the Father to the Son. What the Father does communicate is his creative power (his ἐνεργεια) which makes the Son the intermediary between God and the world of existence. The Holy Spirit comes last and has no divine character.

The decisions of the Councils of Rimini and Seleuciae were strikingly 'hierarchical': "Unicity and Solitude of the Father, Subordination of the Son to the Father, and of the Holy Ghost (minister and servant) to the Son". The Son was declared to be *similar* (ὁμοιος) to the Father without further precision. If the resemblance was neither substantial nor essential, it could only be external.

After long discussions between east and west, the Council of Constantinople restated in 381 a.d. the doctrine proclaimed by the Council of Nicea. The Holy Spirit regained his questioned divinity. The only Son of God is "true God of true God, engendered, but not created, and of the same substance of the Father", the Holy Spirit "emanates from the Father [but not from the Son] and is worshipped and glorified together with the Father and the Son". Let us see how Peirce conceives of the relation of Father to Son.

The Father, himself, is **Ens Necessarium**, and creator of all. But he cannot, as such, act in time, because he is out of time. He "probably has no consciousness" (6.489), except "in a vague sense" (CP 6.508). Thus the *filioque*, the existential necessity of the Son.

Seventy years later, in 451 a.d., the emperor Marcianus summoned the Council of Chalcedon (Kadiköy in Turkey). Marcianus (396-457), the second emperor of the eastern empire, had succeeded Theodosius II (the eldest son of Theodosius I and the author of the Theodosian Code) whose sister Pulcheria he had married. The Council of Chalcedon reopened the question of the relation of the Father and the Son and elaborated the doctrine in order to combat two other errors: that of Nestorius who maintained that there were two persons in Christ: a divine person and a human person (an error which had already been condemned by the Council of Ephesus in 431 a.d.); and that of Eutyches who maintained that there was only one nature in Christ and that was the divine nature. Against Nestorius, the council proclaimed that there was only one person (ὑπόστασις) in Christ and against Eutyches that this unique person has two natures: one divine and one human; Jesus Christ is the Son of God and of Mary.

It may be noted in passing that Tarek Aziz, the present Foreign Minister of Iraq, is a Nestorian, and that Islam maintains that there is only one nature in Jesus Christ, the human nature. Something more important and intriguing is the agreement of 1994 between Pope John Paul II and the Patriarch Mar Dinkha IV, head of the Eastern Assyrian church which is Nestorian, an agreement by which they conjointly declared that "Christ was not a man in the ordinary sense of the word, chosen by God as 'His body' and as somebody to inspire, as it had been the case with the Just and the Prophets, but the very Verb of God, engendered by the Father before all the centuries, without beginning according to His divinity, and born recently from a mother without father, according to His humanity".

This agreement does not solve the mystery of the Trinity. The mystery of the Trinity, which is at the core of the misunderstanding between east and west is still unresolved. In sum:

(1)   For easterners, the mystery is that of one Being (οὐσια) in three *hypostases* (ὑποστάσεις), a formula smacking of Arianism for westerners;

(2)   For westerners, the mystery is that of one Substance (*Substantia*) in three persons (*personae*), a formula redolent of Sabellianism for easterners. Sabellius of Cyrenaica (beginning of the third century) maintained that the distinctions between the persons do not affect the unity of God, because they denote only modes or aspects of God.

3.4 Political Implications

The dispute is not yet at an end and, as before, the theology of the Trinity is the spiritual arm of temporal power. When in the eighth century resistance in Spain against the Arabo-Berber occupiers began to be organized under the influence of the acculturated Visigoths (who had been in power there since the great invasions until 711a.d.), it was in the name of orthodoxy (to which the Visigoth kings adhered only in 589 a.d., having till then been partisans of the Arianist heresy) that the 'resistants' rebelled. They were represented through their spokesman the monk Beatus of Liebana (the author of a famous: *Commentary on the Apocalypse*). The 'collaborators' were personified by Bishop Elipand who preached *Adoptianism*, a variety of Arianism which also denied the consubstantiality of the Father and the Son. This could only be acceptable to the Moslem occupier, since it is the same doctrine as that revealed in the koran: Jesus is a prophet like Moses and Mohammed. Here again the Trinity helped to mobilise the Christians against their enemies. It made possible the reconquest of Spain and the conquest of America (of which Christendom celebrated the 500th anniversary in 1992). America where the Unitarians persecuted in England found refuge in 1620.

3.5 From Greek to Latin

The misunderstanding between east and west concerning the mystery of the Trinity was not only semantic, but syntactic, and probably more a question of culture expressed in two different languages, than a question of theology. The translation from Greek to Latin was the syntactic source of all the confusions which I would explain by the difference between greek and latin cultures: greek culture is philosophical and all of *esprit de finesse*, and latin culture juridic and of *esprit de géométrie*, to use Pascal's distinction. For instance, ὑπόστασις is a good translation of the idea of 'substance' although the latter has a passive connotation in Latin and an active connotation in Greek. But Latin-speakers translated ὑπόστασις (hypostasis) by *persona* (person), which, when added to the translation of *substantia*, changes the greek term οὐσία. For, *persona* denotes an actor's mask and by derivation: role, individuality, person (in grammar). It is only in the second derived sense that *persona* translates ὑπόστασις .

The equalitarian Trinitarism of the west has no origin but the geometrical juridicism of the latin language. And this applies not only to the mystery of the Trinity, but to western philosophy in general when greek philosophy is read in the latin translations of Cicero and reproduced by all the western philosophers. Descartes is as good an example as any as is shown by the American philosopher John Herman Randall:

It is significant that when Descartes asked, "What is Substance?" he was asking for what persists unchanged throughout change, what it is in change that does not itself change. And in Locke and in Kant, in fact, throughout modern philosophy, "substance" has been taken as the unchanging, the permanent in change, whether Locke's "I know not what," or Kant's "permanent in relation to phenomena." But for Aristotle, who since he gave the technical meaning to the term *ousia* rendered into Latin as *substantia*, ought to know, *ousia* or *substantia is* defined precisely as that which undergoes change in change, what is at the end of any process different from what it was at the outset. And in the most important and fundamental kind of change of all, *genesis kai phthora*, "generation" and "corruption," a new *ousia* or substance is present at the end that was not there at all in the beginning, or a substance has disappeared completely. Thus it is clear, Aristotle's pattern of motion and change is a pattern of novelty that emerges in process. (Randall [1960; 112-113])

4. WHY HAS THE MYSTERY OF THE TRINITY NOT SO FAR BEEN SOLVED BY THE CHURCH ?

It will have been noticed that the councils were more concerned with the relation of the Father and the Son than with the question of the Trinity. The Holy Spirit is hardly mentioned except accessorily. Moreover in order to refute Arius, the councils had recourse to a dualistic philosophy: the Aristotelian philosophy of substance.

As already pointed out, to understand the mystery of the Trinity, the mystery must be situated in the politico-cultural context of the time which is that of the opposition between east and west. The Councils of Nicea and Constantinople which imposed the doctrine which is still in force today in the roman church, were summoned respectively by the first and the last emperors of the eastern *and* western empire.

However between these two councils and also outside them and after them, two philosophies are opposed: the Aristotelian philosophy and the Neo-Platonist philosophy, the west favoring the former and the east preferring the latter. It was in an Aristotelian spirit that the Councils of Nicea and Constantinople defined the Trinity: God in three persons *equally* divine.

All the eastern interpretations of the decisions of these councils are Neo-Platonist. I shall note two points of doctrine which are never defended for themselves, but which are ever-present and that we noticed in Peirce's conception of God as triune.

(1)   The conception of a demiurge, the creator of the world, which in the definition of the Trinity becomes that of a solitary Father having no communication with the world, and that of a Son, engendered but not created, creator of the world.

(2)   The Platonist conception of the procession of being.[3]

Schematically, Being, which is inaccessible, has its expression in a process (πρooδoς, translated by the word "procession"), a downward procession in three *hypostases*:

> First *hypostasis*: the One absolute;
> Second *hypostasis*: the One multiple = intuitive intelligence;
> Third *hypostasis*: the One and the multiple = the soul or discursive reason.

It is in this way that the eastern church understands the Trinity: One God in three *hypostases*. Proceeding from God the Father, the Son loses the fullness of being possessed by the Father, but he can communicate with the world - which the Father cannot do. Proceeding from the Father and the Son, the Holy Spirit, without quite losing his divine being (although Eunone maintains the contrary) plunges the divine being into the multiplicity of the empirical world whose foundation is the pure multiple or pure matter.

5. PEIRCE'S SOLUTION

The position that Peirce was to develop is closer to that of Plotinus than that taken by the Councils of Nicea and Constantinople: the Son proceeds from the Father out of time, but precedes him in time. He is a *hypostasis* in the greek sense adopted by the eastern church, not a *substance* in the latin sense of the western church, while possessing both a divine nature and a human nature. The *procession* moves downward: what it gains in multiplicity, it loses in unity: the Father is first, the Son is second, the Holy Ghost is third.[4]

In a letter to his brother Herbert, written before the publication of the neglected argument, Peirce had recognized that the church's conception of

---

3. Plotinus (205-270) from Lycopolis (now Assiout in Egypt), was a commentator of Plato and especially of the: *Parmenides*. Neo-Platonism was born from his commentaries in the famous: *Enneades*.

4. It is to be noted that Peircean Thirdness (discursive reason) is inseparable from pure manifold, but can exist only by the unification (intuitive intelligence) of the manifold, and that the degeneracy is inverted: it is the manifold (God the Father) which is genuine and the unity (the Holy Spirit) which is degenerate in the second degree.

God was close to his own, without entering into details:

> ... various great theologians explain that one cannot attribute *reason* to God, nor perception (which always involves an element of surprise and of learning what one did not know), and, in short, that "mind" is necessarily ... unlike ours, [and] that it is only negatively ... that we can attach any meaning to the Name. (CP 6.502)

References

FISCH, M. [1982] 'Introduction', in: M.H. Fisch *et al.* (eds.) *Writings of Charles S. Peirce: A Chronological Edition, Vol. 1*, Bloomington, IN: Indiana University Press, xv-xxxv.

GORCE, D. [1947] *Pour comprendre la Théologie*, Paris: Douin & Cie.

RANDALL, J. H. [1960], *Aristotle*, New York: Columbia University Press.

INDEX

PRINTED ON PERMANENT PAPER • IMPRIME SUR PAPIER PERMANENT • GEDRUKT OP DUURZAAM PAPIER - ISO 9706

ORIENTALISTE, KLEIN DALENSTRAAT 42, B-3020 HERENT